THE WONDER BOOK OF HORSES

The Wonder Book of Horses

JAMES BALDWIN

LIVING BOOK
PRESS

This edition published 2020
by Living Book Press
Copyright © Living Book Press, 2020

ISBN: 978-1-922348-19-7

A catalogue record for this book is available from the National Library of Australia

CONTENTS

NOTE TO THE READER

The eighteen stories in this volume have been chosen with a thought to their educative value as well as for the intrinsic charm of the original narratives, which in various forms have delighted many generations of readers. All have a literary interest connecting them with subjects with which every educated person is supposed to be familiar. In the first four, you will be introduced to the sun myths and season myths of the Greeks and of our Norse ancestors. Following these, the tale of song-inspiring Pegasus is presented in contrast with that of Griffen, the base imitation invented by the romancing poets of the Middle Ages. Then in "The Ship of the Plains," you may read of the mythical founding of Athens; and in the sketch that follows, you may enjoy a brief glimpse of Arabic imagery in the story of one of the most interesting episodes in the life of the prophet Mohammed. The story of the twin brethren will acquaint you with the thought of some of the old Latin writers, while the tale of Rakush will give you a taste of Persian literature as it is found in the great epic written by Firdusi. The romances of Charlemagne and his peers are represented by the story of Broiefort and his indomitable master; and the world-famous Don Quixote is introduced by his sorry but scarcely less famous steed, Rozinante. The epic of the Iliad is briefly condensed in the biography of Swift and Old-Gold; and the tragic fall of Troy is narrated in the story of the Great Wooden Horse. Then with the Horse of Brass you may-

1

Call up him that left half told
The story of Cambuscan bold;

and finally with Firouz Schah you may take a bold flight into the enchanting regions of romance depicted in the "Arabian Nights' Entertainment."

And so, while you are reading this WONDER-BOOK OF HORSES and finding entertainment in the biographies of winged steeds and war horses, of knights-errant and god-like heroes, you are really doing something more—you are making acquaintance with some of those wonderful and beautiful conceptions which in the form of classic literature have come down to us through the ages.

JAMES BALDWIN

HELIOS'S FOUR-IN-HAND

HELIOS, as you know, was the most famous charioteer that the world had ever seen. Just how long he had been driving the chariot of the Sun nobody could tell; but it must have been many, many years. People said that he had never done anything else; and the oldest inhabitant had no recollection of the time when he began. He never missed a day—not even Sunday; and on holidays he was always up and at it early, cracking his whip cheerily to waken the children. Starting from the home of the Dawn in the far, far East, he made a daily trip to the verge of Old Ocean's stream in the distant West. How it was that he always got back to his starting-point before the next morning was somewhat of a mystery. Nobody had ever seen him making his return trip, and hence all that men knew about it was guesswork. It matters very little to us, however; for that question has nothing to do with the story which I am going to tell.

The old charioteer always slept soundly in the morning, and seldom awoke until he heard his young sister, the maiden whom men call Aurora, rapping at the door of his bedroom, and making her voice echo through the halls of the Dawn.

"Up, up, brother Helios!" she would cry. "It is time for you to begin your journey again. Up, and delight the world once more with your shining morning face and your life-giving presence!"

Then Helios would hasten to the meadows where his steeds were feeding, and would call them each by name:

"Come hither, beautiful creatures! Hasten, for Aurora calleth. Eös, thou glowing one! Æthon, thou of the burning name! Brontë, thou thunderer! Sterope, thou swifter than lightning! Come quickly!"

The wing-footed steeds would obey. The servants would harness them to the golden car, and Aurora and the Morning Star would deck their manes with flowers and with wreaths of asphodel. Then Helios would step into the car and hold the long, yellow reins in his hands. A word from him and the proud team would leap into the sky; then they would soar above the mountain tops and mingle with the clouds, and grandly career in mid-air. And Helios, holding the reins steadily, would gently restrain them, or if they lagged would urge them forward with persuasive words. It was the grandest sight that men ever saw, and yet they never seemed to think much about it—perhaps because it was seen so often. If Helios had failed for a single day, what a wonderful hub-bub and fright there would have been!

The wife of Helios was a fair young lady named Clymene, who lived not far from the great sea, and who, according to some, was a nymph, but according to others a fisherman's daughter: and they had an only son named Phaëthon. Helios loved this son above all things else on earth; and he gave him many rich and noble gifts, and counseled him to be brave and wise, and especially to be contented with his lot in life. And Phaëthon grew to be a tall and comely lad, fond of his looking-glass, soft-handed, and proud of his ancestry. Some of his companions, who were only common mortals, liked to flatter him because of his supposed wealth, while there were many others who despised him because he affected to look up to the Sun.

"See the upstart who calls himself the son of Helios," sneered one.

"Ah, but he will have a sorry fall some of these days," said another.

"You are a pretty fellow to claim kinship with the chari-oteer of the Sun," said a worthless loafer whose name was Epaphos. "With your white face, and your yellow curls, and your slender hands, you are better fitted to help your mother at her spinning than to be a leader of men."

"But," said the boy, "my father Helios, who drives the burning chariot, and who—"

"Don't talk to me," interrupted the unmannerly fellow—"don't talk to me about your father the chariot-driver. Why, you would be frightened to death to drive your sis-ter's goat-cart over the lawn; and you would shriek at the sight of a real horse. How dare you claim descent from the charioteer of the skies? Nonsense!"

"A pretty son of Helios, indeed!" laughed the other rowdies who were with Epaphos; and some young girls that were passing tossed their heads and smiled.

"I will show you!" cried Phaëthon, angrily. "I will do what none of you dare do: I will ride the wild horses of the plain; I will harness them to the king's war-chariot, and drive them in the great circus! I will prove to you that I am worthy to be called the son of Helios!"

"Perhaps you will take his place as driver of the sun-chariot? A day's rest now and then would do the old man great good," sneered Epaphos.

Phaëthon hesitated. "My father," said he, "is one of the

immortals, and I am earth-born. And yet—and yet—"

"And yet," shouted his tormentors, "until you have driven the sun-chariot through the skies, nobody will believe that you are the son of Helios!"

And they went on their way laughing.

"You may sneer, and you may laugh," said Phaëthon, "but the time will come when you will honor me, both for what I am and for what I can do."

Steadily, and with a determined purpose, he set about making himself ready for the great undertaking of his life. He exercised himself daily in feats of strength; he practised running and leaping and throwing weights, until his muscles were hardened and made as elastic as Apollo's bow. Then he took lessons in horsemanship from the greatest riding-masters in the world. He spent months on the grassy steppes of the Caspian, where he learned to lasso wild horses, and, leaping astride of them, to ride them barebacked and bridleless until they were subdued to his will. He entered the chariot races at Corinth, and with a team of four outdrove the most famous charioteers of Greece; and at the great Olympian games he won the victor's crown. No other young man was talked about as much as he.

"A bright young fellow with a brilliant future before him," said some.

"A fine example of what hard work and a little genius can do," said others.

"A lucky chap," said still others—"a mere creature of circumstances. Any of us could do as well, if as many favorable accidents would happen to us to help us along."

"A vain upstart," said those whom he had beaten in the

"AND WITH A TEAM OF FOUR OUTDROVE THE MOST FAMOUS CHARIOTEERS OF GREECE."

race—"a fop with a girl's face, and more hair than brains, whom the gods have seen fit to favor for a day."

"He claims to be of better blood than the rest of us," said the followers of Epaphos; "yet everybody knows that he was born in a miserable village a long way from Athens, and that his mother is the daughter of a fisherman."

But the young girls whispered among themselves: "How handsome he is, and how deftly he managed the reins! What if he be indeed the son of Helios! Wouldn't it be grand to see him sitting in his father's chariot, and guiding the sun-steeds along their lofty road?" And they said to him, "Phaëthon, if you will drive your father's team for only one little day, we will believe in you."

At length Phaëthon made a long journey to the golden palace of the Dawn in the far distant East. Helios, with his steeds, had just returned from the labors of the day, and he was overjoyed to see his son. He threw his arms about him, and kissed him many times, and called him by many endearing names.

"And now tell me," he said, "what brings you here at this quiet hour of the night, when all men are asleep. Have you come to seek some favor? If so, do not be afraid to tell me; for you know that I will do anything for you—that I will give you anything that you ask."

"There is something," said Phaëthon, "that I long for more than anything else in the world; and I have come to ask you to give it to me."

"What is it, my child?" asked Helios, eagerly. "Only speak, and it shall be yours."

"Father, will you promise to do for me that which I shall ask?"

Then Helios lifted up his hands, and vowed by the river Styx which flows through the underworld, that he would surely grant to his son Phaëthon whatsoever he desired. And this he did, knowing full well the terrible punishment that would be his in case he should not observe that vow. Nine years he would have to lie on the ground as though he were dead, and nine other years he would be shut out from the company of his friends; his sun-car would be broken in pieces, and his fleet horses lost forever, and the whole world doomed to everlasting night.

The young man was glad when his father had made this vow. He spoke quickly, and said: "This, then, O father, is the boon which I have come to ask, and which you have promised to give: it is that I may take your place to-morrow, and drive your chariot through the flaming pathway of the sky."

Helios sank back terrified at the request, and for a time could not speak.

"My child," he said at last, "you surely do not mean it. No man living can ever drive my steeds; and although you have kinship with the immortals, you are only human. Choose, I pray you, some other favor."

Phaëthon wept, and answered: "Father, there are some people who do not believe that I am better than mere common men, and they scorn me to my face. But if they could once see me driving the sun-car through mid-air, they and all the world would honor me. And I can drive your steeds; for have I not mastered the wildest horses of the desert, and have I not driven the winning chariot in the Corinthian races? By long years of patient training I have fitted myself for this task."

Through all the rest of the night Helios pleaded with the young man, but in vain: Phaëthon would not listen to any refusal. "This favor I will have or none," said he. "I will drive the sun-car through the heavens to-morrow, and all men shall know that I am the son and heir of Helios."

At length Aurora, in her yellow morning robes, knocked at the door, and Helios knew that no more time could be spent in vain entreaties.

"Ah, my son!" he said, "you know not what you have asked. Yet since I have made the vow I will not refuse you. May the immortals have you in their keeping, and ward all danger from you!"

Then the four horses were led out and harnessed to the car, and Helios sadly gave the reins into Phaëthon's hands.

"Thy folly will doubtless bring its own punishment, my son," he said; and, hiding his face in his long cloak, he wept.

But the young man leaped quickly into the car, and cried out, as his father had been wont to cry: "On, Eös! On, Æthon, Brontë, Sterope! On, ye children of the morning! Awaken the world with your brightness, and carry beauty and gladness into every corner of the earth. Sterope, Brontë, Æthon, Eös, on with you!"

Up sprang the steeds, swift as the thunderclouds that rise from the sea. Quickly they vaulted upward to the blue dome of heaven. Madly they careered above the mountain tops, turning hither and thither in their course, and spurning the control of their driver; for well they knew that it was not their old master who stood in the chariot behind them. Then the proud heart of Phaëthon began to fail within him. He quaked with fear, and the yellow reins dropped from his hands.

"Madly they careered above the mountain tops."

"O my father!" he cried, "how I wish that I had heeded your warning!"

And the fiery steeds leaped upward and soared in the heavens until they reached a point higher than any eagle had ever attained; then, as suddenly, they plunged downward, dragging the burning car behind them; then, for a long time, they skimmed close to the tree-tops, and dangerously near to the dwellings of men. From the valley of the Nile westward, across the continent of Africa, they passed in their unmanageable flight, and the region that had once been so green and fertile was scorched into a barren desert. The rivers were dried up, and the fishes in them died. The growing grain, the grass, the herbs, the trees—all were withered by the intense heat. The mountains smoked, the earth quaked, and the sky was lurid with flame. The fair people who dwelt in that ill-fated land hastened to hide themselves in caves and among the rocks, where many of them perished miserably from thirst and the unbearable heat; and those who survived and came forth again into the light of day were so scorched and blackened that their skins were of the hue of night, and no washing could ever make them white again. Then all living creatures, great and small, cried out in their terror, and besought the ever-living powers to save them from destruction. And mother Gæa, queen of earth, heard them; and, pitying them, she prayed to great Zeus, ruler of gods and men, that he would do something to stop the mad course of the driverless steeds ere the whole world should be wrapped in flames. Zeus, from his palace on high, heard her prayer, and hurled his thunderbolts upon the head of the hapless Phaëthon. The youth, stricken and helpless, fell headlong from the car, and the team of Helios, frightened into obedience, soared aloft to their accustomed pathway, and, though driverless, pursued their journey to the shore of the western ocean. Helios was there awaiting their coming, and when he saw that Phaëthon was not in the car deep sorrow filled his heart; he covered his face with his cloak, and it was long ere his smiles were seen again as of yore.

As for Phaëthon, he fell into the great river Po, and messengers hastened to carry the news of his death into the country of his birth.

And the daughters of the West built him a noble tomb of marble near the shore of the great sea; and they caused an inscription to be engraved upon it, which said that although he had failed in what he had undertaken, yet he was worthy of honor, because he had set his mind on high things.

THE HORSES OF SOL AND MAANE

A VERY long time ago there lived in the far North a man named Mundilfare, who had two children that were famed all the world over for their beauty and grace. The name of the boy was Maane, and that of the girl was Sol, and their father boasted that neither in heaven nor upon the earth were there any beings so fair to look upon as they, so bright of face, so firm of step, so noble in action. Of course his boasting gained for the children no friends, but rather stirred up envy and hatred; and the Asa-folk, who were the mightiest people in that country,—so mighty that they were sometimes called gods,—planned how to get them out of the world. Had Mundilfare been wise, he would have praised the children of the Asa-folk and let people think as they would about Maane and Sol.

The Asas had two horses, noble steeds as yellow as gold and swifter than the storm-winds. They also had a chariot made of hammered gold, in which they had stored by a kind of magic all the sparks that flew up out of the vast fiery region of the South. Once they harnessed the horses to the chariot and sent them out over the earth, driverless and without a guide, to carry light and heat to the nations of men. But the plan was a failure. The horses, wandering whither they pleased, did not serve all parts of the world alike. Some lands were almost burned up with the intense heat that was given out from the car; others were not visited at all, and the people who lived there perished in the cold and the darkness. And so the Asas were upon the point of giving up the scheme entirely; for, although under ordinary circumstances, as in the din of battle or in the roar of the storm, they were the bravest of the brave, yet none of them dared try to drive the golden steeds and the burning chariot. Then one of the wisest among them proposed a plan by which they might kill two birds with one stone, and at the same time bring great honor to themselves.

"This fair maiden Sol and her pale-faced brother Maane," said he, "are, as everybody knows, skilled in the management of horses. Now, let us put the girl into the burning chariot, with the shield Swalin in one hand, and the long, stout reins in the other, and let it be her duty to guide the fiery steeds through the pathway of the skies, favoring all men alike. And let us do likewise with the boy, giving him charge of the feebler team and the silvery chariot, which have stood idle these many years because none of us knew what to do with them. Thus we shall rid ourselves of the hateful boastings of this fellow Mundilfare, and shall confer blessings not a few upon all mankind."

No sooner was this proposition made than all the Asa-folk gladly agreed to it. They took the two children from their homes, and imposed upon each the wearisome task that had been suggested. To Sol they gave the burning chariot, which was henceforth called the sun-car, and to Maane they assigned the silvery car that carried the moon. When fair Sol ascended to her place and took the long golden reins in her hands, the fiery steeds, of whom even the bold Asas were afraid, leaped up into the sky and, under her firm and gentle guidance, journeyed whithersoever she wished. And she named them Arvak and Alswin because they were ever wakeful and as swift as eagles on the wing. But the sparks which flew from the fastturning axle of the sun-car were exceedingly hot and dazzling, and the steeds and their fair driver would have been burned up had not the cool shield Swalin reflected back the heat and sheltered them from the blinding light; nor, indeed, would the horses have been safe even then, had not the Asas hung upon their necks two wind-bags that blew cooling breezes about them all day long and kept them ever fresh and vigorous.

Maane's team was a very gentle one, and he had no trouble in guiding it wherever he wished; and his chariot gave out no heat, but only a soft, silvery light which everybody, and especially children, loved to look upon. Now and then some child who had been very good, or some silver-headed man or sweet-voiced lady, would catch a glimpse of Maane's beautiful face; but it was not often. Once upon a time two children named Juke and Bil—or, as you have it in English, Jack and Jill—went up to their father's well to fetch a pail of water; and the pail was hung from a long pole which they carried on their shoulders. Looking up at the round full moon sailing in the sky, they saw the bright charioteer, and were so charmed by his lovely face that they forgot all about their errand and thought only of the fair vision in the sky above them. And so, wherever Maane drove his team, there they went also, careless of their burden and thoughtless of the bumps and falls which they got in running after the moon. Maane, who had been watching them all the time, was touched by their devotion to him, and finally, after they had wandered very far from home, he drove his team close down to the earth and lifted them into the car beside him. And now, any bright night when the moon is full, you may see Jack and Jill in it, with the pole lying on their shoulders and the pail of water still hanging below it; for they never, never tire of admiring the beauty of their master's face.

The life of Sol and Maane was not an unhappy one, for they loved the horses which they guided, the one daily, the other nightly, over the vaulted blue roof of the sky. There was not much that happened anywhere on the earth without one or the other of them seeing it. For when Sol sank to rest in the great sea, or drove her fiery steeds down behind the western hills, Maane would start out with his feebler team and drive silently onward among the clouds and the troops of stars—silently lest he should waken the sleeping earth. But his sleek-coated horses were never able to keep pace with Arvak the ever-wakeful, and Alswin the eagle-chaser, which drew his sister's car; and so, even if they started together, he was sure to fall steadily behind, little by little, every day, until at the end of four weeks Sol would gain upon him one entire trip. Then, when she passed him in her swift car, he would hide his face in his long cloak because of the dazzling sunlight, and the two would begin the race over again. But it always ended the same way: Sol would make twenty-eight trips to Maane's twenty-seven.

But by and by, when the Asas had been almost forgotten, a wise man came into the world, who spent all his time in looking at things through a glass, and in writing long rows of figures in a little book, and in putting everything at right angles on shelves instead of letting them lie around loose.

He looked at the sun-car and the moon-car through his glass, and declared that he saw neither horses nor drivers, nor indeed any wagons, but only the sun and moon. But there is no wonder that he did not see them, for his eyes were not of the right kind, nor his heart either, for that matter. Then he set out to prove by figures that the sun always stands in the same place, and that the moon is too big to be put into a wagon of any kind; and, after much talking, he succeeded in making a great many people think that he knew more about such things than did the charioteers themselves, or even the Asa-folk, who had started the whole affair. Of course Sol and Maane did not care to stay in the business after they found that the world was losing faith in them, and so they went into retirement, as people would say nowadays—that is, they turned their steeds about and drove their chariots into the safe and pleasant country of Fairyland, where all such creations of the fancy find refuge.

THE BLACK STEEDS OF AIDONEUS

THEY lived for the most of the time in a land of dread, deep down in the earth, where the light of the sun could not reach them; and that, it may be, is what made them so dark. Men said that they were as black as coal, as ink, as tar, as the ace of spades. But they were so strong and swift and proud, and their eyes were so bright, and their coats were so sleek, that no one could see them and not wish to have them for his own. And yet so sharp of tooth, so light of heel, so full of fire were they, that it would have been worth your life to touch them. King Aidoneus kept them in stalls of gold that he had built for them near the banks of the stream which is called the Styx, and there he fed them and cared for them with his own hands.

Since in all his realms there was no light of the sun, nor smiles of friends, nor joy of life,—naught but tears and the shades of night,—Aidoneus liked at times to come up to the world of love and hope to see what kind of cheer he might find there. And so now and then men caught sight of him in a cloud-like car drawn by his four coal-black steeds, which flew through the air with the speed of the wind, or pranced and reared on the edge of some steep cliff, or leaped down from the top of some far-off height. And the tales which they told of his deeds were such as fill the heart with fear; for they said that his breath was cold as the blast of the north wind, or else hot as the fire that leaps from Mount Etna's mouth; and cloud and storm, and hail and snow, and dire pain and dread—all these he brought to the earth in the wake of his swift car and night-black team.

Now one day in the late fall, when the frost had not yet touched the leaves, and the fields were still bright with bloom, he thought that he would ride out and see some of the fair things that had been born of the earth and the sun. He rode up by way of Mount Etna, and out through the smoke and clouds that poured from its top, and looked down toward the green fields of Enna, not far from its base. Then, with a sharp word to his team, he drove in great haste down the steep slopes, and paused not till he reached the plain.

Some girls who lived near the foot of Mount Etna had gone out to spend the day in the fields, and with them was a fair young maid named Persephone, the child of Dame Demeter. The sun was warm, the sky was fair, the grass was soft. The girls, free as the wild birds of the wood, ran here and there, and dreamed of no harm. At length Persephone, tired of play, sat down on a stone to rest; but the others went on, and were soon out of sight. Then all at once she heard a strange sound as of huge wheels and the tramp of hoofs, and ere she had time to run home to the safe arms of Dame Demeter, a black car drawn by four coal-black steeds was at her side. In the car stood a tall, sad-faced man, who wore a crown of gold on his head. Persephone screamed and stood still—it was all that she could do. Then she was caught up in the strong arms of Aidoneus, who, swinging his long whip in the air, cried out to his steeds:

"On, Eton, thou who art swift as birds on the wing! On, Nonios, thou whom no flash of light can outspeed! On,

Abatos; no storm is so fleet as thou, no thought can run so fast! On, Abastor; race thou with the stars that shoot through the sky! Speed ye all! Speed ye all! "

And the wild steeds, urged thus by lash and speech, flew through the air, as it were, and climbed up, up, up the steep slopes of Etna, and paused not till they stood on the edge of the great black cup and the flue whence smoke and blue flames came up from the dim depths of Aidoneus's realm. Poor Persephone shrieked, and tried to leap out of the car; but the stern old King soothed her fears with kind words, and told her that so long as she would stay with him she should be safe from harm. Then a sheet of flame shot up and shut out the light of day, and the steeds, the car, the King, and the maid went down, down, down, and were seen no more.

When the news was brought to good Dame Demeter that her child was lost, she did not faint nor cry out in her great grief and fear, for she was too brave and wise for that. But she went out at once in search of the maid, and vowed that she would find her or come back no more. With a black veil wound round her head, and with a torch in her hand, she crossed the seas, and went from land to land, and asked all that dwelt on the earth if they had seen her child. For a whole year she searched in vain. Then she thought that she would go to Helios, him who drives the sun-car through the skies, and ask him.

"Great Helios," she said, "I know that your eye takes in all the world, and that the deeds of both gods and men are known to you. Tell me, I pray you, have you seen my lost child Persephone?"

Kind Helios was glad that she had come to him. Yes, he

had seen Persephone. As chance would have it, he had seen Aidoneus when he rushed out from Etna; he had seen him lift the child from the ground and place her in his black car; he had seen the last wild leap down Mount Etna's throat.

"She is with Aidoneus," said he; "and he has made her the queen of his dark realms. But he would not have seized her as he did had he not had leave of Zeus, the king of gods and men."

Then Dame Demeter gave way to her grief and rage; and she sent word to Zeus that no fruits nor grain should grow in all the world so long as Aidoneus kept Persephone in his halls. For it was Dame Demeter, men said, who gave life to the trees and plants, and made them bloom and bear fruit. Zeus and the gods that were with him knew that the dame would be as good as her word, and the thought filled them with fear. If there should be no food for men, save flesh and fish, they would soon be as wild as they were in the old, old time, and would care naught for the gods.

"It is hard to have to give up to her whims," said great Zeus; "but the best that we can do is to fetch Persephone back to her."

And so he bade Hermes, him who had the winged feet, to go down to the halls of Aidoneus and bring the lost maid back.

Aidoneus was glad to see Hermes, but he frowned when he learned why he had come.

"Do you not know the law?" he asked.

"What law?"

"There is a law which none of the gods—no, not yourself, nor even Zeus—can break. I will read it to you." And he took a black book from the shelf on the wall, and, when he had found the place, read these words:

*"That one, be it god or man, maid or child, who tastes food
while in the realms of Aidoneus, shall not go out therefrom
so long as the world stands."*

Then Hermes asked Persephone if food had passed her
lips since the day that Aidoneus had brought her to his
halls. And the maid told him that she had been too sad to
think of food; yet once, as she stood on the bank of the
Styx, she had plucked some bright red fruit that grew there.

"Did you taste it?"

"Yes, I took just one small bite, and then threw it far
from me."

Aidoneus clapped his hands with glee.

"What kind of bright red fruit grows on the banks of
the Styx?" asked Hermes.

"Pomegranates," said the King.

"But what is a pomegranate?" asked Hermes. "It is a
poor kind of food. At the best, not more than one third of
it is fit to eat. The rest is skin and seeds."

And so he took Persephone back to Dame Demeter, and
said that for eight months of each year she should live on
the glad green earth; but that for four months Aidoneus
might claim her as his queen. Hence it is that so long as the
grains of corn lie dead in the ground, Persephone stays in
the drear realms of Aidoneus. But when the stalks begin
to grow and the buds of the fruit trees to burst, then the
sad-faced King comes in his dark cloud-car, drawn by his
four night-black steeds, to bring Persephone back to Dame
Demeter's door. And there the fair maid lives all through
the spring and the warm months of the year, till at last the
chill days of the late fall bring snow and ice and hoar frost.
Then comes Aidoneus on the wings of the storm-cloud,

with Eton, swift as birds, and Nonios, quick as light, and Abatos, fleet as thought, and Abastor, who outspeeds the stars. And they bear the maid up Etna's slopes, and are lost to sight in the smoke and blue flames.

And now each year, when the leaves fall and the days grow cold, dark clouds are sure to come. They hide the sky and chill the air and drive joy from the fields and woods. You may see them as they sweep along, blown by wild gusts of wind, with snow and hail and driving sleet in their train.

Do you know what these clouds are? Look and you will see.

They are, in truth, the four black steeds of Aidoneus, and the dark car, and the sad-faced King; and they bear Persephone to the shades deep down in the earth. But in four months there-from the sun will call; the seeds in the ground will sprout and grow; the buds will swell and burst; the dark clouds will come with the winds, as of yore, but this time they will bring life in their train. The fair Queen will come home in the car that is drawn by the four black steeds of Aidoneus.

BAS-RELIEF FROM AN ARCH IN ROME.

THE EIGHT-FOOTED SLIPPER

DID you ever hear of the curious riddle which old-fashioned people in the North used to tell one another on Wednesday mornings? It was something like this:

"Who are the two that ride over the rainbow? Three eyes have they together, ten feet, two arms, and a tail. And thus they journey through the world."

You can't guess it, and it will be of no use for you to try. But all those old-fashioned people knew the answer; and everybody repeated the question to everybody else, not as a puzzle nor to gain information, but simply because it was the custom, and therefore the right thing to do. In that respect it was like the briefer and more matter-of-fact riddle which people propound to one another nowadays: "It's a fine morning, isn't it?" But it didn't mean the same. The answer which everybody gave to everybody was this:

"The two who ride over the rainbow are Odin and his steed Sleipnir. Odin has one eye, the horse two; the horse runs on eight feet, Odin has two; two arms has Odin, and the horse has a tail."

A horse with eight feet would of course have many advantages over the commoner kind that have only four. If a heavy load had to be drawn, only think what a wonderful leverage his long legs would give him! If a long journey were to be taken, how nicely he could hold up half of his feet and give them a rest while the other four were steadily jogging along! And then in racing and jumping, what an impetus all those legs, working together, would give him! Many tales are told of his prowess and of the feats which he performed, but I will repeat to you only one—the famous story of his journey to the underworld.

There was great grief in the house of Odin, for word had been brought that Balder, his best-loved son, was dead. Balder, the white, the pure, the good, the fair, had been treacherously slain, and all the world was in mourning. Who now would bring good gifts to men? Who would bless them with smiles and sunlight, as Balder had done? Out by the shore of the sea the people had gathered to perform the last sad rites for the dead hero. Balder's own ship, the *Ringhorn*, had been drawn up on the beach, and in it were placed all the most precious things that had been his. The deck was piled with cedar-wood, and between the layers of sticks were placed gums and rich spices and fragrant leaves, and the whole pile was covered with fine robes, and a couch was made whereon to lay the body of the dead. Then Balder's horse, Gyller the Golden, was led on board, saddled and bridled as if for a long journey. His arms also were brought—his shield and sword and bow and quiver— and laid by the side of the couch. Finally the hero himself was borne to his last resting-place, and Nanna, his young wife who had died of grief, was laid beside him. The great ship was pushed into the sea and set on fire. Wrapped in flames and hidden by dense clouds of smoke, it drifted far away from the shore.

"Alas! alas! " cried the people, "what will become of us, now that Balder is dead—now that the sunlight is gone out of the world?" And they went to their homes weeping, and sat down in the darkness and cold, and could not believe that aught of joy would ever come to them again.

And other things sorrowed, too. The trees bent their heads, and the leaves upon them fell withered to the ground. The meadows doffed their green summer coats and dressed themselves in sober suits of russet. The birds forgot to sing. The small creatures of the woods hid themselves in the ground or in the hollow trunks of the trees. The cicadas no longer made merry in the groves. The music of the busy world was hushed. Nowhere could be heard the sound of the spindle or the loom, of ax or flail, of the harvesters' song, of the huntsmen's horn, of the warriors' battle-cry; but only the dull thud of the waves beating against the shore, or the wild whistling of the winds among the dead branches of the trees.

In the King's high halls Balder's mother lamented his untimely fate, and his sisters were beside themselves with grief. Odin, with his blue hood pulled down over his face, sat silent in the twilight and listened to the moaning of the sea. He was not only troubled because of the death of his son, but the sadness of the world oppressed him. What if the universal grief should continue and joy never return? Frost and ice and darkness would at length overwhelm the earth, and the race of mankind would perish.

"We must bring lost Balder back to us!" he cried. "He must not stay in the gloomy halls of the under-world. And yet how can we persuade Hela, the pale-faced Queen of that region, to give him up? "

"Hela is deaf to prayers," answered one of his councilors; "and, moreover, she will be glad to keep the bright Balder in order that perchance some joy may be known to the dwellers in her own domains. And yet, mayhap, if some one of your own household shall go down and carry your prayers to her, she will relent and give him up."

"Ah, so she may!" cried the Queen-mother. "But who among his brothers will dare undertake so fearful a journey?"

"I will dare!" cried Hermod, Balder's younger brother. He was only a little fellow, but he was famous all over the world for the quickness of his movements and for his horsemanship. "I will go down to Hela's house with your prayers, if only I may ride Sleipnir, who is both fleet and sure-footed."

Gray Sleipnir was at once led out and saddled with the greatest care; and food and drink were given him, enough for eighteen days. Then Hermod, booted and spurred, sprang upon him and rode fearlessly away along the shadowy highroad that leads toward the land of the stern-faced Hela. Nine days through mists and fogs, nine nights amid darkness and unseen perils, did the good steed gallop steadily onward; and his eight iron hoofs, clattering upon the rocky roadway, roused strange echoes among the barren hills and frowning mountain passes. Nine days and nine nights did bold Hermod sit in the saddle with his face bared to the chilling winds and his heart set firm upon his errand. Many were the sad-eyed travelers whom they overtook, all journeying toward the same goal, but not one did they meet returning. And pale specters flitted in the air above them, and ogres grinned in the darkness, and owls hooted from the clefts of the rock. But none of these things could frighten Sleipnir; for were not the mystic runes of Odin engraved on his teeth? And no terror could make Hermod falter; for was not his errand one of love and mercy?

At length, having passed through a dark and narrow valley where there were many unknown and fearful things, they came out upon a broad plain which is the beginning of the great silent land. A dim yellow light illumined the sky, and the air seemed soft and mild, and a restful peace abode there. But no sound of any kind was heard; even the striking of Sleipnir's hoofs upon the pavement was noiseless; and when Hermod tried to sing, he found that he could not hear his own voice. On the farther side of the plain they carne to a broad river that flowed silently toward the sea. It was the river Gjol, and across it was the long Gjallar Bridge, a narrow roadway roofed with shining gold. Here Sleipnir slacked his pace, and Hermod found that the great silence had been left behind. At the end of the bridge was a gate behind which stood a maiden named Modgud, whose duty it was to take toll of all the travelers who passed that way.

"Who are you," she asked, "who ride so heavily across the frail Gjallar Bridge, and what kind of beast is that which you bestride?"

"I am Hermod, of the house of mighty Odin," was the answer; "and this beast is Sleipnir the Glider, the fleetest and the wisest of all horses."

"Why do you ride so hard, and why are you so wondrous heavy?" asked the maiden. "Never have I seen this golden bridge shake and sag as it did under your weight. Only yesterday five thousand passengers were crowded upon it at once, and yet it trembled not in the least. Surely you are not the kind of man that should travel this road. There is too much color in your face, and too much strength in your arm. Why do you ride into the land of Hela?"

"I am on my way to Hela's halls to find my brother

Balder," answered Hermod. "He has but lately passed this way, and I doubt not but that among all the multitudes who have given you toll you remember him."

"Indeed, I do remember him. Two days ago he came, riding his good steed Gyller the Golden, and his sweet-faced wife Nanna was beside him. Never before did such brightness cross this river; never before did beauty such as his pass over into the land of Hela. If you will promise to bring him back this way, I will lift the gate and allow you to ride on, for I see you have nothing to give me for toll."

"I promise," said Hermod. "But which way shall I ride to find Hela's halls?"

"The way lies downward and northward," answered Modgud. "It is not far, and you cannot miss the road. Farewell!"

Hermod gave the word to Sleipnir, and the horse galloped swiftly onward down the steep way that the maiden had pointed out. In a little while they came to the walls of a huge castle that stood gloomy and dark among the hills. On the outside was a deep moat filled with water. The drawbridge was up and the gate was shut. Hermod tried to call to the watchman, but the sound of his voice died away before it left his mouth. He looked around in the hope that he might attract the notice of some one in the towers or on the walls. But there was not a soul in sight. At length he dismounted and gave Sleipnir a good breathing spell, while he measured with his eye the distance to the top of the castle wall. Then he stroked the horse's gray mane, read the runes on his teeth, and whispered them in his ear. At last he carefully tightened the saddle-girths and remounted.

"Good Sleipnir," he said, "you have borne me thus far, and have not failed me. Stand me in stead this one time,

I bid you. Let those eight long limbs of yours be wings as well as legs!"

Then, at a touch of the spur, Sleipnir sped with lightning swiftness down the narrow roadway toward the edge of the moat, and in another moment was flying through the air right over the gate and into the courtyard beyond. It was a wonderful leap; but then it was a wonderful horse that made it. No sportsman's trained hunter ever cleared ditch and hedge with half the ease and grace that great Sleipnir cleared the high wall of Hela's castle. Safe within the courtyard, Hermod alighted and tied the horse to an iron post that stood by the side of a fountain. Then, seeing that all the doors were open, he walked boldly in without asking leave of anyone, and made his way to the long banquet-hall where Hela and her guests were feasting. Whom should he see, sitting in the foremost seat at the Queen's right hand, but his brother Balder! The light which shone in Balder's countenance and glittered in his eyes shed a soft radiance over the entire hall, such as its gloomy walls had never seen before; and the faces of the guests were wreathed in smiles, and the Queen herself seemed to have forgotten all her sternness. Hermod, unbidden though he was, was welcomed very kindly, and a seat was given him at the table. All that evening he mingled with the guests in the hall. He talked with his brother, or told wondrous stories in the hearing of the Queen, but not once did he speak of the business upon which he had come.

The next morning, when he thought that Hela was in her pleasantest mood, Hermod asked whether Balder might not ride home with him to his sorrowing mother, whose heart would be broken if he did not return.

"Does she weep for him?" asked the Queen.

"Yes, and not only she, but my father and his counselors, and our brothers and sisters—all the household of Odin weep."

"There are so many such households that, if weeping availed anything, I should soon be deprived of all my subjects. There is no home that does not weep for its loved ones."

"But all mankind weeps for Balder."

"All mankind? Well, if that be true, there is some reason for your request, but not enough."

"All living creatures mourn for him," added Hermod.

"Indeed! But I should weep if you were to take him away from me. Do things that are lifeless also grieve for him?"

"Truly they do. The very rocks shed tears, as do also the mountains and the clouds. There is nothing that does not weep."

"Do you know that this is true? Will you swear it?" asked the Queen, earnestly.

Hermod hesitated. "I am quite sure that it is true," he finally answered. "But, not having seen everything, I cannot now make oath to it."

"I will tell you what I will do," said Hela. "Do you return to your home, and let Odin send into all the earth and find out for a truth whether everything really weeps for Balder. If he shall find that this is the case, then come to me again, and I will give your brother up. But if a single thing shall refuse to shed tears, then Balder shall stay with me."

Hermod was not altogether pleased with this answer, but he knew that it was useless to plead any further with the Queen, and so he took leave of her, and made ready to return. Balder took from his finger a precious golden ring, and gave it to him to carry to Odin as a keepsake; and

Nanna sent a kerchief of green and some flowers to her mother. Then Hermod mounted good Sleipnir again and rode back, along the fearful way, out of the land of Hela, and came on the tenth day to Odin's palace.

There was, of course, still greater grief in the King's household when it was seen that Hermod returned alone. But when he made known the conditions on which Hela would give Balder back to them, all were glad, for they felt sure that, at the worst, it would be but a few months until they should see his bright face again.

And so messengers were sent into all the world, praying that everything should weep for white Balder. And everything did weep—men and beasts and birds, trees and plants, rivers and mountains, sticks and stones, and all metals. At the end of a year the messengers returned, very glad to report the result. But just before reaching Odin's halls they passed the mouth of a cavern wherein sat a toothless old hag named Thok. They asked her kindly to weep for Balder. She shook her head, and mumbled between curses:

"Bah! Why should such as I weep? Little good did he ever do me; little good will I do him. Go and tell him to stay where he is."

The joy of the messengers was turned to sadness, and with bowed heads they went up the hill whereon Odin's palace stood, and told the whole story.

When kind Hela heard, however, that not anything save the wicked hag had refused to weep for Balder, she was moved to be better than her word. For she consented that Balder, for six months in every twelve, might gladden the earth with his presence. But during the other six she would keep him in her own halls. And this is why the sun shines, and the trees are green, and the birds sing, and men rejoice from April to October, for that is the season of Balder's stay with them; but during the other months the sun seldom shows his face, and all things are silent and sad, because Balder has gone back to the under-world.

But we must not forget the good steed Sleipnir. Although he never made another journey to the under-world, there was scarcely any part of the earth to which his long legs did not sometimes carry him; and especially in the far North he was a familiar figure long after Odin had gone from the earth.

In some parts of Sweden the old horse had, until quite recently, a troublesome habit of running through the harvest fields and making sad tangles of the standing grain. But by and by the cunning farmers learned a trick that saved them from all further trouble. As soon as the oats or barley was tall enough they would cut and tie up a fair sheaf of it, and lay it high up on a fence where the frolicsome old fellow would be sure to see it before getting into the field.

"Ah! how kind the dear farmer is to provide this sheaf of sweet barley for me," Sleipnir would say to himself. "I really cannot have the heart to tangle his grain." And then he would gallop away to the next farm. Wednesday night was—and still is, for all I know—his favorite time for visiting the fields; for Wednesday, as you know, is Odin's day. And that, I suppose, is the reason why people always selected Wednesday as the best time in the week for puzzling one another with the question:

"Who are the two that ride over the rainbow?"

THE WINGED HORSE OF THE MUSES

I. THE FOUNTAIN OF THE HORSE

PEOPLE said that the gods sent him to the earth. Of course it was very desirable to account in some way for the appearance of so wonderful a creature, and there was no easier way to do it. But to this day nobody knows anything about his origin. When first seen he was simply a beautiful horse with wings like a great bird's, and he could travel with equal ease in the air and on the ground.

A good many years ago—so many that we shall not bother about the date—this wonderful animal, after a long and wearisome flight above the clouds, alighted at a pleasant spot near the foot of Mount Helicon, in Bœotia. He was hot and thirsty, and having seen some reeds growing at that spot, he hoped that he would find there a stream of water, or at least a small pool, from which he could drink. But to his disappointment there wasn't a drop of water to be seen—nothing but a little patch of boggy ground where the tall grass grew rank and thick. In his anger he spread his wings and gave the earth a tremendous kick with both of his hind feet together. The ground was soft, and the force of the blow was such that a long, deep trench was opened in the boggy soil. Instantly a stream of water, cool and sweet and clear, poured out and filled the trench and ran as a swift brook across the plain toward the distant river. The horse drank his fill from the pleasant fountain which he himself had thus hollowed out; and then, greatly refreshed, unfolded his wings again and rose high in the air, ready for a flight across the sea to the distant land of Lycia.

Men were not long in finding out that the waters of the new spring at the foot of Mount Helicon had some strange properties, filling their hearts with a wonderful sense of whatever is beautiful and true and good, and putting music into their souls and new songs into their mouths. And so they called the spring Hippocrene, or the Fountain of the Horse, and poets from all parts of the world went there to drink. But in later times the place fell into neglect, for, somehow, people were so busy with other things that they forgot the difference between poetry and doggerel, and nobody cared to drink from Hippocrene. And so the fountain was allowed to become choked with the stones and dirt that rolled down from the mountain; and soon wild grass and tall reeds hid the spot from view, and nobody from that day to this has been able to point out just where it is.

II. THE YOUNG TRAVELER

But the horse?

We left him poised high in the air, with his head turned toward the sea and the distant land of Lycia. I do not know how long it took him to fly across, nor does it matter; but one day, full of vigor and strength, and beautiful as a poet's dream, he alighted on the great road that runs eastward a little way from the capital city of Lycia. So softly had he descended, and so quietly had he folded his great wings and set his feet upon the ground, that a young man who was walking thoughtfully along the way did not know of his presence until he had cantered up quite close to him.

The young man stopped and turned to admire the beautiful animal, and when he came quite near reached out his hand to stroke his nose. But the horse wheeled about and was away again as quick as an arrow sent speeding from a bow. The young man walked on again, and the horse soon returned and gamboled playfully around him, sometimes trotting swiftly back and forth along the roadway, sometimes rising in the air and sailing in circles round and round him. At last, after much whistling and the offer of a handful of sweetmeats, the young man coaxed the horse so near to him that by a sudden leap he was able to throw himself astride of his back just in front of his great gray wings.

"Now, my handsome fellow," he cried, "carry me straight forward to the country that lies beyond the great northern mountains. I would not be afraid of all the wild beasts in Asia if I could be sure of your help."

But the horse did not seem to understand him. He flew first to the north, then to the south, then to the north again, and sailed hither and thither gaily among the white clouds. At the end of an hour he alighted at the very spot from which he had risen, and his rider, despairing of making any progress with him, leaped to the ground and renewed his journey on foot. But the horse, who seemed to have taken a great liking to the young man, followed him, frisking hither and thither like a frolicsome dog, not afraid of him in the least, but very timid of all other travelers on the road. Late in the afternoon, when they had left the pleasant farm-lands of Lycia behind them and had come to the border of a wild, deserted region, an old man, with a long white beard and bright glittering eyes, met them and stopped, as many others had already done, to admire the beautiful animal.

"Who are you, young man," he inquired, "and what are you doing with so handsome a steed here in this lonely place?"

"My name is Bellerophon," answered the young man, "and I am going by order of King Iobates to the country beyond the northern mountains, where I expect to slay the Chimæra, which lives there. But as for this horse, all I know is that he has followed me since early morning. Whose he is and from whence he came I cannot tell."

The old man was silent for a few moments as if in deep thought, while Bellerophon, very weary with his long walk, sat down on a stone to rest, and the horse strolled along by the roadside nipping the short grass.

"Do you see the white roof over there among the trees?" finally asked the old man. " Well, under it there is a shrine to the goddess Athena, of which I am the keeper. A few steps beyond it is my own humble cottage, where I spend my days in study and meditation. If you will go in and lodge with me for the night, I may be able to tell you something about the task that you have undertaken."

Bellerophon was very glad to accept the old man's invitation, for the sun had already begun to dip below the western hills. The hut contained only two rooms, but everything about it was very clean and cozy, and the kind host spared no pains to make his guest comfortable and happy. After they had eaten supper and were still reclining on couches at the side of the table, the old man looked Bellerophon sharply in the face and said:

"Now tell me all about yourself and your kindred, and why you are going thus alone and on foot into the country of the Chimæra."

III. BELLEROPHON'S STORY

"My father," answered Bellerophon, "is Glaucus, the king of far-off Corinth, where he has great wealth in horses and in ships; and my grandfather was Sisyphus, of whom you have doubtless heard, for he was famed all over the world for his craftiness and his fine business qualities, that made him the richest of men. I was brought up in my father's house, and it was intended that I should succeed him as king of Corinth; but three years ago a sad misfortune happened to me. My younger brother and I were hunting among the wooded hills of Argos, and we were having fine sport, for we had taken much game. We had started home with our booty, and I, who was the faster walker, was some distance ahead of my brother, when, suddenly, a deer sprang up between me and the sun. Half-blinded by the light, I turned and let fly an arrow quickly. The creature bounded swiftly away, unhurt, but a cry of anguish from the low underbrush told me that I had slain my brother.

"Vainly did I try to stanch the flow of blood; vainly did I call upon the gods to save him and me. He raised his eyes to mine, smiled feebly, pressed my hand as in forgiveness, and was no more.

"I knew that I dared not return home, for the laws of our country are very severe against any one who, though by accident, causes the death of another. Indeed, until I could be purified from my brother's blood, I dared not, as you know, look any man in the face. For a long time I wandered hither and thither, like a hunted beast, shunning the sight of every human being, and living upon nuts and fruits and such small game as I could bring down with my arrows. At length I bethought me that perhaps old King Prœtus of Tiryns, in whose land I then was, might purify me; or if not, he might at least slay me at the altar, which would be better than living longer as a fugitive; and so, under the cover of night, I went down into Tiryns, and entering the temple with my cloak thrown over my head, knelt down at the shrine where penitent men are wont to seek purification.

"I need not tell you how the king found me and puri-fied me and took me into his own house and treated me for a long time as his own son; it would make my story too long. . . . But a few weeks ago I noticed that a great change had come over him, for he no longer showed me the kind attention which I had learned to expect of him. The queen, too, seemed to have become my enemy, and treated me with the haughtiest disdain. Indeed, I began to suspect that she was urging her husband to put me out of the way, and I should not have been surprised if he had banished me from his court. I was, of course, uncomfort-able, and was trying to think of some excuse for leaving Tiryns, when the king, very early one morning, called me into his private chamber. He held in his hand a wooden tablet, sealed with his own signet, and he seemed to be greatly excited about something.

" 'Bellerophon,' he said, 'I have written on this tablet a letter of very great importance, which I wish to send to my father-in-law, King Iobates, of Lycia, beyond the sea. You are the only man whom I can trust to carry this letter, and so I beg that you will get ready to go at once. A ship is in the harbor already manned for the voyage, and the wind is fair. Before the sun rises you may be well out at sea.'

"I took the tablet and embarked, as he wished, without so much as bidding good-by to any of his household. A good ship and fresh breezes carried me over the sea to Lycia, where I was welcomed most kindly by your good king Iobates. For he had known both my father and my grandfather, and he said that he owed me honor for their sakes. Nine days he held a great feast in his palace, and all the most famous philosophers, merchants, and warriors were invited to his table, in order that I might meet them and hear them talk. I had not forgotten the tablet that King Prœtus had given me, and several times I had made a start to give it to Iobates; but I knew that it would be bad taste to speak of business at such a time. On the tenth day, however, after all the guests had gone home, he said to me:

" 'Now tell me what message you have brought from my son-in-law Prœtus and my dear daughter Anteia. For I know that they have sent me some word.'

"Then I gave him the tablet. He untied the ribbon which bound the two blocks of wood together, and when he had broken the seal he lifted them apart and read that which was engraved on the wax between them. I do not know what this message was, but it must have been something of great importance, for the king's face grew very pale, and he staggered as if he would fall. Then he left the room very quickly, and I did not see him again until this morning, when he called me into his council-chamber. I was surprised to notice how haggard and worn he was, and how very old he seemed to have become within the past three days.

"Young man,' he said, speaking rather sharply, I thought,—

'Young man, they tell me that you are brave and fond of hunting wild beasts, and that you are anxious to win fame by doing some daring deed. I have word, only this morning, that the people who live on the other side of the northern mountains are in great dread of a strange animal that comes out of the caves and destroys their flocks, and sometimes carries their children off to its lair. Some say it is a lion, some a dragon, and some laugh at the whole affair and call it a goat. I think myself that it must be the very same beast that infested the mountain valleys some years ago, and was called by our wise men a Chimæra; and for the sake of the good people whom it annoys, I should like to have it killed. Every one to whom I have spoken about it, however, is afraid to venture into its haunts.'

" 'I am not afraid,' said I. 'I will start to the mountains this very hour, and if I don't bring you the head of the Chimæra to hang up in your halls, you may brand me as a coward.'

" 'You are a brave young man,' said the king, 'and I will take you at your word, but I would advise you to lose no time in starting.'

"I was surprised at the way in which the king dismissed me, and the longer I thought about the matter the stranger it all seemed. But there was only one thing to do. I walked out of the king's palace, found the shortest road to Mount Climax, and—here I am!"

IV. THE DREAM AND THE GIFTS

"Do you have any idea what it was that King Prœtus wrote to King Iobates?" asked the old man.

"Why should I?"

"Then I will tell you. He wrote to say that you had been accused of treasonable crimes in Tiryns, and that, not wishing to harm you himself, he had sent you to Lycia to be put to death. King Iobates was loath to have this done, and so he has sent you out against the Chimæra, knowing that no man ever fought with that monster and lived. For she is a more terrible beast than you would believe. All the region beyond the mountains has been laid waste by her, hundreds of people have been slain by her fiery breath alone, and a whole army that was lately sent out against her was routed and put to flight. The king knows very well that she will kill you."

"But what kind of a beast is this Chimæra?" asked Bellerophon.

"She is a strange kind of monster," was the answer. "Her head and shoulders are those of a lion, her body is that of a goat, and her hinder parts are those of a dragon. She fights with her hot breath and her long tail, and she stays on the mountains by night, and goes down into the valleys by day."

"If I had only a shield, and my bow and arrows, and could ride the good winged horse whithersoever I wished him to go, I would not be afraid of all the Chimæras in the world," said Bellerophon.

"Let me tell you something," said the old man. "Do you go out to the little temple in the grove before us and lie down to sleep at the foot of the shrine. Everybody knows that to people who are in need of help Athena often comes in dreams to give good advice. Perhaps she will favor you with her counsel and aid, if you only show that you have faith in her."

Bellerophon went at once to the little temple and stretched himself out on the floor close to the shrine of the goddess. The winged horse, who had been feeding on the grass, followed him to the door, and then lay down on the ground outside.

It was nearly morning when Bellerophon dreamed that a tall and stately lady, with large round eyes, and long hair that fell in ringlets upon her shoulders, carne into the temple and stood beside him.

"Do you know who the winged steed is that waits outside the door for you?" she asked.

"Truly, I do not," answered Bellerophon. "But if I had some means of making him understand me, he might be my best friend and helper."

"His name is Pegasus," said the lady, "and he was born near the shore of the great western ocean. He has come to help you in your fight with the Chimæra, and you can guide him anywhere you wish if you will only put this ribbon into his mouth, holding on to the ends yourself."

With these words, she placed a beautiful bridle in Bellerophon's hands, and, turning about, walked silently away.

When the sun had risen and Bellerophon awoke, the bridle was lying on the floor beside him, and near it were a long bow with arrows and a shield. It was the first bridle that he had ever seen—some people say that it was the first that was ever made—and the young man examined it with great curiosity. Then he went out and quickly slipped the ribbon bit into the mouth of Pegasus, and leaped upon his back. To his great joy, he saw that now the horse understood all his wishes.

"Here are your bow and arrows and your shield," cried

the old man, handing them to him. "Take them, and may Athena be with you in your fight with the Chimæra!"

V. THE FIGHT WITH THE CHIMÆRA

At a word from Bellerophon, Pegasus rose high in the air, and then, turning, made straight northward toward the great mountains. It was evening when they reached Mount Climax, and quite dark when they at last hovered over the spot which the Chimæra was said to visit at night. Bellerophon would have passed on without seeing her, had not a burning mountain sent out a great sheet of flame that lighted up the valleys and gave him a plain view of the monster crouching in the shadow of a cliff. He fitted an arrow quickly in his bow and, as Pegasus paused above the edge of the cliff, he let fly directly at her fearful head. The arrow missed the mark, however, and struck the beast in the throat, giving her an ugly wound. Then you should have seen the fury of the Chimæra, how she reared herself on her hind feet; how she leaped into the air; how she beat the rocks with her long dragon's tail; how she puffed and fumed and roared and blew her fiery breath toward Pegasus, hoping to scorch his wings or smother both horse and rider with its poisonous fumes. Bellerophon, when he saw her in her mad rage, could no longer wonder that the whole country had been in terror of her.

"Now, my good Pegasus," he said, stroking the horse's mane, "steady yourself just out of her reach, and let me send her another keepsake!"

This time the arrow struck the beast in the back, and instead of killing her, only made her more furious than ever. She attacked everything that was in her reach, clawed the

"PEGASUS ROSE HIGH IN THE AIR."

rocks, knocked trees down with her tail, and filled all the mountain-valleys with the noise of her mad roarings. The third arrow, however, was sent with a better aim, and the horrid creature, pierced to the heart, fell backward lifeless, and rolled over and over down the steep mountain side, and far out into the valley below.

Bellerophon slept on the mountain that night, while his steed kept watch by his side. In the morning he went down and found the Chimæra lying stiff and dead in the spot where she had rolled, while a score of gaping countrymen stood around at a safe distance, rejoicing that the monster which had laid waste their fields and desolated their homes had at last been slain. Bellerophon cut off the creature's head, and remounting Pegasus, set out on his return to King Iobates.

Of course old Iobates was astonished to see Bellerophon come back with the monster's head in his arms. All that he did was to thank the young hero for the great service which he had done for his country; and then he began to study up some other means of putting him out of the way.

At length, Bellerophon bethought him that, since this world was beset with so many distressing things, worse even than Chimæras, he would leave it and ride on the back of Pegasus to heaven. There is no knowing what he might have done, had not Zeus, just in the nick of time, sent a gadfly to sting the horse. Pegasus made a wild plunge to escape the fly, and Bellerophon, taken by surprise, was tumbled to the earth. Strange to say, the hero was not killed, but only blinded by his fall; and he never heard of Pegasus again.

GRIFFEN THE HIGH FLYER

I. THE WIZARD OF THE PYRENEES

OLD Atlantes, the wizard of the Pyrenees, had built a tower for his laboratory on the topmost peak of a gray mountain. There was no magic about the tower at first—only solid walls of masonry with one narrow door and, at the top, a dome of glass, where the sage could sit and gaze at the stars. But the wise wizard hoped that by the exercise of his art he would be able to bring magic out of the place by-and-by. And so, if you could have looked in upon him on any fair night or rainy day, you would have seen him surrounded by retorts and alembics, and pots and vials, and wands, and magic circles and books, and signs of the zodiac, and the thousand and one things necessary to the wizard's trade. Scattered about the room, in no very orderly manner, were bundles of all kinds of herbs, ingots of gold and silver, thin sheets of tin and copper and zinc, curiously-shaped bits of colored glass, rolls of wire, and many a strange instrument and tool, the uses of which were known only to Atlantes himself. Sometimes the people in the valley below saw thick clouds of black smoke coming out of the chimney of the wizard's den, as they called it; and belated travelers, groping along the highway on dark nights, reported that they had seen sheets of flame and balls of red fire shooting from the high tower.

Atlantes had not been long in his lofty perch before he was the terror of all the country round about. When he ventured down into the valley, the poor folk who saw him would cross themselves and mutter prayers to the Virgin and look at his feet to see whether they were not hoofed. Men would go miles out of their way rather than venture along the highroad that ran directly beneath his aery; and strange tales were told of children and knights and ladies that had been spirited away by his enchantments and held in captivity by him. But old Atlantes cared little for what people said about him, so long as they did not disturb him in his studies and experiments.

Like other alchemists, he hoped that his experiments would some day lead him to the discovery of the philosopher's stone, which would transmute all the baser metals into gold, and hence the most of his studies were directed to that end. He thought that, if he could only get the smallest vialful of the fluid called lightning, and mix it with some other ingredients which he had at hand, the secret would be within his grasp. But how to obtain the lightning-fluid was the puzzle—and having obtained it, how could he control it until the mixture should be effected?

One night, when a great storm was raging in the mountains, and the thunder was rolling from peak to peak, and flashes of lightning filled the air with terror, he tried a very odd experiment which he had been thinking of for a long time. He understood very well the terrible nature of the lightning-fluid in its free state, and hence he was wise enough not to risk bringing it into his laboratory until it was properly confined. He had arranged, therefore, for trying the experiment at some distance from his tower. There he had hewn a deep cavity in the rock, within which he now placed a huge jar and several pots containing some objects the names of which he would never disclose. I think that among them there were several strips of copper and zinc, a solution of potash, a bar of soft iron bent into the shape of a horseshoe, and possibly some other things now well known to electricians. At any rate, he arranged them very carefully, and having laid a slab of marble over the cavity, went back to his tower to await what might happen.

In the morning the storm had cleared away, the sky was cloudless, and the wizard, as he stepped from his door, could hear the peasants singing in the harvest-fields far over the hills. When he called to mind the experiment of the night before, he smiled at his ludicrous folly, as it now seemed to him. And yet, curious to know what the storm might have done with his magic mixture, he went out and lifted the marble slab. Had a flash of lightning really issued from the cavity, he could not have been more astounded. For, from the urn wherein he had placed, as I suppose, the zinc and the copper, and the potash solution, there sprang a white horse with great wings, from which the sunlight reflected all the colors of the rainbow.

Any other man would have been much more astounded than Atlantes. But you must know that he was acquainted with all the lore of the ancients, and he recognized the horse at once as the modern descendant of Pegasus, the carrier of the thunderbolts of mighty Zeus. He was happier than if he had really discovered the philosopher's stone. He called the horse Griffen, and the airy creature submitted itself at once to his mastership.

II. THE CASTLE IN SPAIN

And now the wizard, with the aid of his winged steed, began to build a marvelous castle of magic among the mountains of Spain. The structure was finished in a day and a night, and, viewed from the plains below, it appeared to be as beautiful as a dream and as delicate and ethereal as the white clouds of a midsummer day.

The country people were not more surprised to see the shining walls and lofty turrets looming up from the hitherto barren summit of the mountains than they were astounded at the unwonted sight of a horse winging its way in mid-air with the white-bearded wizard seated on its back. Knights and soldiers riding through the country wondered what feudal lord had built his stronghold so high above the plain; but, search as they would, they could find no road nor even so much as a pathway by which any one could ascend to it. Nobody would have been surprised to see the castle disappear as suddenly as it had come into being; but there it stood day after day, its roof and battlements gleaming in the sunlight, and the blue smoke rising from its tall chimneys. It seemed to have come to stay.

But what was the use of a noble castle without any noble men or fair women to live in it? If Atlantes had been less wise, this question would have given him some concern; but he had built the palace for inhabitants, and he understood exactly how to encourage immigration into his territories. He might have filled his halls with phantoms bred of his own fanciful dreams and as unsubstantial as the castle itself; but he was too much of a realist for that. He was himself a creature of flesh and blood, of brawn and brains, and he felt that only men and women of the same persuasion were fit to enjoy the delights of his airy palace. To obtain the kind of guests which he preferred, therefore, he had recourse to a cunning stratagem.

Early every morning, with his great spectacles astride his nose and a big book in his hands, he would mount his winged horse and soar out over the country to some spot where a noble cavalier or a fair, high-born dame would be likely to pass during the day. There he would wait until his unsuspecting victim drew near, when the horse would suddenly alight and block up the road. Then the wizard, still sitting in his saddle, would begin to read aloud from the book. At the sound of the very first word, the knight or fair lady would forget everything that had ever happened before, would forget home, friends, and name, and think only of the honey-sweet tones that issued from the magician's lips. When the last words were pronounced the victim would come meekly forward, and, being lifted upon the pillion behind Atlantes, would be firmly strapped to the saddle. Then the good horse would spread his rainbow wings, and carry his double burden to the great air-castle on the Spanish mountain.

Thus the wizard filled his halls with the nobility of France and Spain. Nobody who once entered the golden gateway cared to go out again: each one lived in utter forgetfulness of his past life, thinking only of the delights of each passing hour. He could not even recall his own name, and he never thought of asking for the names of others.

Everything was done that could be done for the comfort and amusement of the wizard's guests. In the great courtyard was a fountain playing in a huge marble basin supported by crouching lions. Beyond it were pleasure gardens filled with flowers and fruits. The interior of the palace was in keeping with its marvelous exterior. The floors were of marble or were covered with the softest carpets, the walls were hung with the finest tapestry, the ceilings glittered with many a gem. Soft couches invited everyone to rest. The sweetest music floated on the perfumed air. The tables in the dining-hall were loaded with delicacies. Servants moved hither and thither, attentive to every call. What mortal would wish to awaken from such dreams of enchantment, to return again to the world of war and bloodshed and toil and trouble?

III. THE FOILED ENCHANTER

It is altogether possible that Atlantes would have robbed all Europe of its chivalry and beauty, had not something occurred to put an end to his schemes. But as it often happens to mice and men, so also did it happen to the wizard. The fact is that he had grown tired of sallying out every day on Griffen's back in search of new guests, and so he had planned another way of entrapping unwary cavaliers into his prison-house. After much labor and thought he cleared away a narrow bridle-path from the highroad at the foot of the mountain to the gates of his castle at the summit. The lower end of this pathway was hidden in a thicket close by a gushing spring of water, and so cunningly was the whole thing constructed that nobody, looking up from below, would notice the smallest sign of a path; and yet if knight or footman once entered the hidden road, he could follow it with the greatest ease to the end.

Old Atlantes, like a spider in his den, sat in his high towers and kept a sharp lookout for his prey. Whenever he saw any knight riding along the highroad who appeared to be worthy of becoming his guest, he devised some means of enticing him to enter the bridle-path. After that, of course, it was very easy to persuade him to ascend until he had safely entered the great trap that had been set for him at the top. This new scheme seemed to succeed wonderfully well, and in a short time there was scarcely a horseman of any note in all Spain who had not fallen into the snare.

It so happened one warm day in summer that a famous English traveler named Astolpho stopped at the spring to rest and to bathe his hot face in the flowing stream. He rode a beautiful black horse named Rabican, which the King of Cathay had lately given him as a token of his esteem. This horse he left in the shade of some trees at a little distance from the road, while he returned to the spring to quench his thirst. He laid his spear and shield down upon the ground, and by them placed the heavy helmet that he had lifted from his head. Then, on hands and knees, he leaned over to drink. But scarcely had his lips touched the water, when a noise caused him to look around.

A gawky countryman had loosened Rabican and was in the act of leaping upon his back. Astolpho quickly seized his spear and ran to save his horse and take the thief. But the rogue was not so easily captured. He entered the bridle-path and urged the horse up the steep ascent. Astolpho followed, always upon the point of laying hold of the horse, but always just a little too far behind. Soon he was surprised to find himself at the top of the mountain and at the very entrance to the great white castle whose towers he had seen and admired from below. The gate was open, as if beckoning him to enter, and Rabican and his rider had already disappeared within. Astolpho, not minded to lose so good a steed, ran boldly onward into the courtyard.

Some knights were there, pitching horseshoes, but they were so busy with their game that they did not notice his entrance. He looked into the banquet hall. A number of lords and ladies were seated about the table, feasting and making merry. He ran into the garden. There was no Rabican there. He peeped into the cellars. Hogsheads of wine and barrels of beef and pork were ranged about the walls, and red-faced kitchen servants were running here and there; but there were no signs of either the horse or the thief. He asked a lubberly boy to show him the way to the stables, but the fellow merely stared at him and made no answer. As he went into the courtyard again, an old man with long, flowing beard came out with a book in his hand and began to read.

But Astolpho, too, had a book—a book which a prince of India had given him, and which he always carried with him— and he was proof against all enchantments of that kind. He knew at once that he had been entrapped in a magic castle, and without heeding the wizard in the least, he turned to his own book to learn from it how he might escape. It was a kind of guidebook to all the houses of enchantment in the world, and he soon found the chapter that was devoted to the air-castles of Spain. The directions were very plain:

"HOW TO FOIL THE ENCHANTER AND SET HIS PRISONERS FREE. *Raise the white stone slab that lies beneath the doorway. The spirit that is pent beneath will escape and the palace will go up in smoke.*"

It was all very simple, certainly. Astolpho had no trouble in finding the white stone, and he began prying it up with his spear. Atlantes, greatly alarmed, cried out to the watchman to open the gate and let the intruder go; and in order to drive him out he tried all the new enchantments that he could think of. The guests, hearing the unwonted uproar, came crowding out to see what new thing had been invented for their amusement. All wore curious colored glasses that the wizard had given them, and to each of them Astolpho appeared in a different form. To one he seemed a giant; to another a dragon; to a third an ugly dwarf; and to still another a savage beast. All with one purpose rushed upon him with swords and sticks and stones, anxious to drive him away from their palace of pleasure.

It would have gone hard with Astolpho, had he not thought of a magic horn which he wore suspended by a gold chain about his neck. It was the gift of a famous enchantress, and was worth a thousand swords. He put it to his lips and blew a single blast. The sound was so fearful that Atlantes and all his guests and servitors took to their heels, and hastened to hide themselves in the inner chambers of the palace. It was then but the work of a few moments for Astolpho to raise the white stone. It revealed the entrance to a spacious chamber in which were a thousand curious things—burning lamps, magic circles, golden bridles, and the like—and at the farther end, tethered by a golden cord, was our old friend Griffen, fully caparisoned with saddle and bridle, ready for a flight among the clouds. What was Rabican compared to such a steed as this? Astolpho lost no time in leading him from the chamber.

At the very moment that Griffen emerged from the

underground chamber, a clap of thunder rent the air, and lo! the wonderful palace of enchantment disappeared. Not one sign of the beautiful structure was left to show where it had stood. The barren rock, which formed the summit of the mountain, was as smooth and clean as if it had been swept by the winds and polished by the hail. And there were the knights and fair ladies who had so lately been the guests of Atlantes, standing bewildered and frightened and cold on the very edge of the dizzy cliff. Soon, as if by instinct, they turned about and filed sadly and silently down the narrow bridle-way to the plain. Once safely on the highroad, they betook themselves their several ways, but neither their memory nor their proper senses came back to them until each had reached his own home.

As for old Atlantes, he skulked down the mountain, and made his way on foot across the country to the high-built tower in the Pyrenees, where he was when we first met him. And there, I have been told, he was content to stay for the rest of his life, busy among his retorts and alembics and herbs and minerals and signs of the zodiac.

IV. THE FLIGHT TO THE MOON

And Griffen? You should have seen how proudly he soared into the sky with brave Astolpho on his back. He and his master became famous as the greatest travelers of their time. Distances were nothing to them. Mountains and seas and broad rivers were no barriers to hinder them. At one time they journeyed northward above the vineyards and fields of fair France, and stopped for an hour in Paris, where Charlemagne was then reigning in the height of his power. There Astolpho learned that Orlando, the noblest of the men of his time, had lost his senses and had wandered away to Africa, or somewhere else, in search of them.

Astolpho set off at once to find him, resolved that he would never rest until he had brought the lost hero back to France. And so the gallant Griffen winged his way back toward Spain; he hovered for a few minutes above the wizard's high-built tower, while his rider consulted with Atlantes about the direction he should take; he turned eastward and skirted the vine-clad hills of Provence; he floated high above the snow-clad Alps, and neighed shrilly as he passed over Genoa, nestled between the mountains and the sea; he dropped one of his quills in Florence, and whinnied with delight as he saw the City of Seven Hills sleeping beneath him; and, all the time, Astolpho sat astride of him, with pen in hand, inditing wonderful stories of his adventures in foreign lands.

They alighted only when they were hungry, for the horse never tired, and Astolpho had only to look at a city to know all about its history, its people and their customs, its public buildings and its laws, and whether any demented knight was wandering about its streets. Leaving Italy, they passed over the Mediterranean, flinging down another quill at Malta, and throwing side glances toward Athens and Constantinople. Speeding over old Egypt, from north to south, Astolpho read the history of thirty centuries in the Pyramids, and wise Griffen solved the mystery of the Sphinx. Finally, after topping the Abyssinian mountains, they alighted in the mythical land of Prester John, and Astolpho at once introduced himself to that wise monarch, and stated the business which had brought him thus to the very ends of the earth.

"Great king," he said, "we had in our country a knight, noble, and brave, and kind, who in an unlucky moment had the misfortune to lose the greater part of his senses. I have searched for them in every nook and corner of the known world, but, alas, I cannot find them. The unfortunate knight himself is at this moment somewhere in the Dark Continent, useless alike to himself and his country. As a last resort I have come to you, knowing how wise you are, to ask whether there are not some superfluous senses lying about, unclaimed, in your kingdom."

"That is a fine horse that you ride," said the king. "He must be a swift traveler."

"He is very fleet, indeed," answered Astolpho. "Why, sir, he can girdle the earth in forty minutes."

"Then, how long would it take him to fly to the moon?"

"He has never been there, but I suppose it would not require very long—say, not more than twenty minutes—half as long as to go round the earth."

"Then, if you are willing to make the journey," said Prester John, "I doubt not but you will find there the thing that you are looking for. For the moon, you must know, is the attic chamber of the world, and everything that is lost finds its way there sooner or later. Lost pins, lost stitches, lost opportunities, lost sheep, lost time, lost causes, lost money, lost senses—they all go to the moon, where the three weird Sisters bottle them up and label them, and lay them on the shelf till called for. There is only one thing that is never given back again, no matter how loudly its owner demands it."

"What is that?"

"Lost time," said old Prester, solemnly; "and I would

advise you to lose none of it if you would go to the moon to recover your friend's senses."

Astolpho, taking the hint, threw himself astride of Griffen, and the horse soared aloft toward the full moon, which had just risen, round and bright, above the eastern hills.

But why should I weary you with the story of that marvelous flight? And why need I tell you how the brave Astolpho found Orlando's senses just as the wise king had said he would? Neither would you care to hear how Griffen winged his flight back to the earth again; nor how his master searched through darkest Africa until he had found his demented friend; nor how Orlando took his recovered senses as a child takes nauseous medicine; nor how good Griffen, with proud Astolpho on his back, finally wended his way over the sea and land to the noble island of Britain. I will not tell you of any of these things, nor of any of the later journeys of the two famous travelers. For you will find the whole story truthfully narrated in the books which Astolpho wrote with a pen plucked from the gallant Griffen's wing.

THE SHIP OF THE PLAINS

HE was the first real flesh-and-blood horse of which we have any account. Some men say that he was the first animal of the kind that ever lived, but this is doubtful. Snowy white, without spot or blemish, from the tips of his ears to the tips of his amber hoofs, how he must have astonished the simple-minded folk of Cecropia when he leaped into their midst right out of the earth at their feet! If you should ever go to Athens and climb to the top of that wonderful hill called the Acropolis, look around you. You may see the very spot where it all happened. But to the story.

Did I say that the people who lived there at that time were simple-minded? Rather childlike they were in some ways, and not so worldly-wise as they might have been had they lived several thousand years later; but they were neither simpletons nor altogether savages. They were the foremost people in Greece. It was all owing to their king, wise old Cecrops, that they had risen to a station superior to that of the half-wild tribes around them. He had shown them how to sow barley and wheat and to plant vineyards; and he had taught them to depend upon these and their flocks and herds for food, rather than upon the wild beasts of the chase. He had persuaded them to lay aside many of their old cruel customs, had set them in families with each its own home, and had instructed them in the worship of the gods. On the top of the Acropolis they had built a little city, and surrounded it with walls as a protection against attacks from their warlike neighbors; and from this point as a center they had, little by little, extended their influence to the sea on one side and to the mountains on the other. But, strange to say, they had not yet given a name to their city, nor had they decided which one of the gods should be its protector. They had been so busy, learning and doing, that they had had no time to think about such matters.

On a certain day in autumn, after the grain had been harvested and the grapes had been gathered and made into wine, two strangers suddenly appeared in the market-place. Nobody knew whence they came, nor how they had climbed the steep pathways and entered within the walls unseen by the guards. The man, dark haired, huge-limbed and strong, bore as his only weapon a trident, or three-pronged harpoon, made of bronze. The woman was tall and stately, with large, round eyes and long hair that fell in ringlets about her shoulders, and she wore a gleaming helmet upon her head, and carried a bright, round shield upon her arm.

"What is the name of this city?" asked the man, speaking to the wondering people in the market-place.

"It has no name," answered one of the wisest among them; "but we sometimes call it Cecropia, or the city of Cecrops, the king who founded it and is its ruler. The country round about us is called Attica, because it is bounded on three sides by the sea."

"But where is your temple?" asked the woman. "And which of the gods is your city's patron and guardian?"

"Truly, we have but lately learned that there are any gods," was the answer; "and we render homage unto them all. If we knew which one of them would bless our people with the richest gifts, that one should be our patron and guardian, and to that one we would rear a temple. But how shall we know?"

"Do but lead us into the presence of the king," said the strange man, "and the matter shall be decided at once."

It happened that at that very moment King Cecrops was seated in his chair of state at the gate of the market-place, where he was wont every morning to listen to the petitions of his people and to dispense justice to rich and poor alike. When the two strangers were led into his presence he was so struck by their majestic appearance that he arose and received them standing, and in tones of humility and respect bade them make known their names and their errand.

"My name," said the woman, "is Athena, and it is I who give men wisdom and skill, and teach them the arts of peace and instruct them in all manner of handicraft. Make me the patron and guardian of this beautiful new city that you have builded, and its fame and that of the people who dwell therein shall be remembered to the end of time."

"Not so!" cried her companion. "I am Poseidon, the strong, the ruler of the sea, the shaker of the earth, and I claim this city for my own. Would you be rich and power-ful, with fleet ships upon the sea and great armies upon the land? Would you make yourselves feared by all the nations of the earth? Then accept me as your patron, and build me a temple here upon your Acropolis!"

"Which shall it be, my people?" asked King Cecrops of the multitude that had gathered around. "Which shall we choose for our city's heritage, "Wisdom or Strength?"

"Wisdom!" cried some. "Strength!" cried others. And

there was great confusion. Finally, an old man with white hair and very long white beard made himself heard.

"It seems to me, O King," he said, "that we should choose that one for our patron and guardian who can give us the most substantial blessings. We are a new people, and as yet we know so little of either Wisdom or Strength that we are not qualified to judge which is best. But let Athena and Poseidon each give us something, now and here, as a sample of the blessings which they promise us, and do you, O King, with your twelve councilors, decide which has offered the better gift; and then we will choose that one to be the patron and guardian of our city, and to that one we will build a temple here on our Acropolis."

"It is well!" cried the king.

"It is well!" cried Athena and Poseidon.

"It is well!" echoed the people.

"And do you agree?" asked the king, addressing the rival claimants.

"We agree," said they both. "We submit to the trial at once; and do you and your councilors decide which of our gifts is the more acceptable."

Then Poseidon strode haughtily forward and smote the bare rock with his trident. So heavy was his stroke that the entire hill trembled beneath it, and a deep, narrow cleft was opened in the solid limestone. Then out of the fissure there leaped a snow-white horse with flashing eyes and arching neck and impatient feet. It was the most wonderful creature that the people had ever seen, and they were terribly frightened by his sudden appearance.

"Behold the horse!" said Poseidon. "Behold the noblest of all beasts, man's best friend, the emblem of power and strength and of your own glorious future with me as your patron and protector."

Then Athena touched the ground with her shield, and forthwith there sprang out two tiny green leaves; and to these two other leaves were added, and then others and others, until a slender twig appeared. Then the twig grew into a spreading tree, with clusters of flowers and rich, oil-producing fruit; and birds built their nests among the branches, and children gamboled in the shade beneath.

"Behold the olive tree!" said Athena. "It is my gift to you, and the emblem of the blessings that I will confer upon your city."

The king and his councilors sat for a long time in silence, looking now upon the beautiful but terrible animal, and now upon the tree with its fruit and flowers and inviting shade. The horse was by far the most attractive object that they had ever seen, and the longer they looked upon him the more their wonder grew.

"What will we do with him now that we have him?" asked one.

"Will he feed the hungry?" asked another.

"Truly, he will be but an expensive luxury to us," said a third, "and not nearly so great a blessing to our people as the olive tree."

And so they rendered their decision. Poseidon's gift, they said, was a noble one, a wonderful one; but Athena's was preferable because it promised the most substantial blessings to all the people.

"Athena shall be our patron and protector!" cried they.

"And the name of our city shall be Athens, and we are henceforth Athenians!" cried all the people. And they

"SWIFT AS THE WHIRLWIND."

forthwith began to clear the ground for the erection of that world-renowned temple, the ruins of which still crown the summit of the Acropolis. And Athena took up her abode with them.

As for Poseidon, he strode out of the gates in great rage, and the hill shook again under his heavy footsteps as he descended to the plain. He loosed all the winds and sent them hurtling against the walls of Athens, and for twelve days there were storms on sea and land the fiercest that men had ever seen. But what had those to fear who had chosen Wisdom for their protector and friend?

The wonderful steed which Poseidon had brought out of the rock was a greater terror than the storm, and the good people were glad to open the city gate and allow him to depart. Having descended into the fields, he tossed his head proudly, kicked his heels high into the air, and set off at great speed toward distant Thessaly and the vast pasture lands of the North. The men of Athens watched him in his flight across the plain. Swift as the whirlwind, with his long mane floating gracefully over his back, he looked not unlike some white-sailed vessel scudding before the wind across the ruffled surface of the sea. The people had been at a loss to find a name for the strange creature, but they caught eagerly at the suggestion that now offered itself.

"See!" cried one, "is he not a ship, a skiff with sails?"

"He is the Ship of the Plains!" said another.

"Yes, we will call him Skyphios, or the Ship of the Plains!" cried they all.

And men afterward said that it was from Skyphios that the wild horses of the Scythian desert—nay, of all the world—are descended.

AL BORAK

AL BORAK — the name is Arabic, and means The Lightning. And this is the story which faithful Moslems tell of the wondrous steed.

It was midnight, thirteen hundred years ago, and Mohammed, the prophet, lay asleep in his house in the ancient city of Mecca. Suddenly he was roused by hearing a loud voice crying: "Up, up, thou sleeper! Arise and make ready for thy journey!"

Mohammed leaped to his feet and looked about him. Before him stood a creature of dazzling radiance whom he took to be an angel. His face was white as the purest marble, his hair was of gold and fell in silk-like waves about his shoulders, his wings reflected all the colors of the rainbow, and his robes of spotless white were embroidered with gold and thickly set with precious gems.

Mohammed was about to speak when he saw that the angel was holding the reins of a steed the most marvelous that any man ever beheld. It appeared to be a horse, and yet it was not like a horse. Its limbs were slender and long, its body was strong-built and finely formed, its coat sleek and glossy, and its mane so long that it almost swept the ground. Its color was white, intermingled with golden-yellow, and there was a golden star in its forehead. Folded over its back were wings like those of an eagle, amid the plumes of which the lightning gleamed and flashed. Its eyes were brighter than coals of fire, its ears were sharp-pointed and restless, its nostrils were wide, blood-red, and steaming. It had the face of a man, although the cheeks of a horse, and it spoke with a human voice in the purest Arabic.

Mohammed had no sooner seen this wonderful steed than he was filled with a desire to mount it. But when he reached forth his hand and made ready to spring upon its back, it reared high in the air, and would have struck at the prophet with its golden hoofs had not the angel restrained it.

"Be still, Borak!" cried the latter. "Do you not know who this is whom you oppose? It is Mohammed, the son of Abdallah, of one of the tribes of Arabia the Happy. He is the prophet of Allah, and it is through his intercession only that any creature can enter paradise."

Al Borak at once became as gentle as a lamb, and her eyes were filled with beseeching tears as she turned to the prophet and said:

"O thou, the most honored of mortals, I pray thee that thou wilt intercede for me!"

"Be assured that I will," answered Mohammed; "for never was steed more worthy of paradise than thou art!"

Then Al Borak allowed the prophet to mount upon her back, and, rising gently from the ground, she soared aloft above the desert sands and mountains of Arabia. The night was dark—the darkest that any man ever knew; and it was so still that all nature seemed sleeping and dead. There was no sound anywhere of stirring wind or of rippling water. No chirp of wakeful insect, no rustle of creeping reptile, no baying of dogs, no howling of wild beasts among the mountains, disturbed the solemn hour. All Arabia was silent as the grave. And Al Borak, with face directed northward, and at a speed which outdistanced thought, sailed noise-lessly through the gloom.

Only thrice did the steed alight upon the earth—first upon Mount Sinai, then in the village of Bethlehem, and finally at the gate of the temple in Jerusalem. There Mohammed dismounted, and, fastening the steed to a ring which was attached to one of the stones of the temple, he left her and went in. But I need not speak of what happened to him there, nor of his further journey, nor of whom or what he saw; for those things have naught to do with Al Borak. When, at length, he returned to the gate of the temple, he found the steed in the place where he had tethered her, and, having remounted her, he was carried in an instant back to Mecca and set down at his own door. Then Al Borak, having bowed low in honor of the prophet, unfolded her wings again and soared aloft into the upper air, never again to be seen by mortal man.

The distance from Mecca to Jerusalem is about eight hundred miles as the crow flies, or as Al Borak flew. And yet, although Mohammed had not stopped at Jerusalem, but had gone some millions of miles beyond, the whole affair was accomplished in less time than you can think of it. It is easy to prove that this was so. In the first hurry of setting out, a vase of water had been overturned by the angel's wing; but Mohammed returned in time to catch the falling vessel before its contents could be spilled. Could anything have been quicker? Not even thought or a flash of light could have outsped Al Borak.

THE GREAT TWIN BRETHREN

LET us imagine ourselves in Rome on the fifteenth day of July, two thousand years ago. It is a public holiday, and as all the Roman *equites* are out on horseback, we may see many of the finest war-horses that the world could at that time produce. A brilliant company of riders, starting from the temple of Mars outside the ancient walls, wind their way through the main streets of the city, and finally, crossing the Forum to its southeastern corner, draw rein in front of the stately building dedicated to the memory of Castor and Pollux.

The entire course over which they pass is decked with gay banners, flowers are strewn in their way, and they are greeted at every turn with loud shouts of joy and approval. You notice that these knights are not clad in armor, but in flowing robes of purple, and their brows are encircled with wreaths of olive. Garlands of flowers also hang about the necks of their horses and from the reins and saddle-bows; and companies of Roman maidens march in front of them, singing songs of the deeds of the dauntless heroes who lived in the brave days of old. When they reach the end of their route, the noblest men of Rome, the patricians, senators, and consuls, welcome them from the steps of the temple, and the entire Forum echoes with the shouts of the people.

There are also ceremonies, perhaps sacrifices, being performed within the temple, but we do not care to inquire about them—we only want to know what is the meaning of this holiday. There are multitudes of fine horses on exhibition, but this is clearly no horse show. The flower of the Roman cavalry is in the procession, but it is plainly no grand review of troops. The—

But let us ask the old veteran who sits sunning himself in the portico of the temple of Saturn across the way.

He is astonished that we should make such an inquiry, and he looks upon us with suspicion. But he is a garrulous sort of fellow, and is glad of any chance to use his tongue, and so he answers us civilly.

"You must be strangers in Rome," he says, "or you would know that on this day every year —the ides of Quintilis, we call it—the equites hold a festival in honor of the Great Twin Brethren, the patrons of their order. Two hundred times or more have we thus celebrated the anniversary of the victory which they won for the Roman people in the hard-fought battle of Lake Regillus."

We ask him to tell us all about the Twins, and his astonishment at our ignorance is greater than before. Nevertheless, as we sit beside him on the floor of the portico, he kindly relates this story:

IT happened a very long time ago, only twelve years after the Roman republic had been founded. The last of the kings, old Tarquin the Proud, was still living—an exile among our enemies, the Latins—and he was all the time plotting to get back. Thirty cities had finally united and raised a great army in order to force our people to restore him to the throne. It was, indeed, a trying time, and the fate, not only of Rome, but of the world hung upon the issue.

Thirty against one was great odds, so far as numbers were concerned—but what are thirty jays against a royal eagle?

The dictator, Aulus Postumius Albinus, hastened to go out and give battle to the enemy on their own ground. Every able-bodied man in Rome was with him—some fully armed, but many with only such weapons as they could snatch up from among their working tools—scythes, axes, pitchforks, flails, and the like. Nobody was left to defend the walls except the small boys and the decrepit old men, under the command of a noble ancestor of mine named Sempronius Atratinus. They might almost as well have been left without defenders, but then, of course, nobody intended that the enemy should ever come so near to the city.

All this space in front of us, on the right of the great roadway which we call the Via Sacra, was at that time open ground. It was used as a pasture for the cows and the geese, and the children from the hills on either side often went out there to play. Over there, where now stands the temple of Castor and Pollux, was a gushing spring of clear, cold water, surrounded by a pond where the cattle came in the heat of the day, and the barelegged boys fished for minnows and sailed their tiny boats.

Well, two days had passed since the Roman army had marched out to meet their foes, and no word had come back to the city. Sempronius was becoming very anxious. Since early in the morning he had been in the watch-tower straining his eyes eastward. Far away toward the Apennines he fancied he saw the dust of battle rising in faint, misty clouds above the hills, but he could make sure of nothing. He would have sent out a messenger to learn how the day was going with our people, but there was not a horse left within the walls, and who among the feeble folk that were with him could undertake so difficult an errand? On either side of him, on the wall and above the gate, were the old men who had been left behind, together with many of the Roman matrons and maidens, all eager to know the issue of the day, and all listening if they might be the first to hear the sound of horse-hoofs galloping from the field of fight.

Meanwhile some children playing around the pond were astonished, on lifting their eyes, to see two monstrous white horses drinking from the spring, and on their backs were two men clad in snow-white armor that glistened strangely in the sunlight. There were splotches of blood all over the horses, and the white armor was stained in many places with mud and red gore.

With shrieks of fright the children fled across the fields, and the news of what they had seen was soon carried to the watchers above the gate. Scarcely believing their story, Sempronius, followed by a wondering company of women and boys, hastened down to see for himself. There, indeed, were the snow-white steeds standing by the spring, and there were the two riders who, having dismounted, were washing them in the clear water.

So like were the two horses that no man living could tell one from the other. So like were the two warriors in face and form and movement that no point of difference between them could ever be discovered.

"What news bring you from the battle?" cried Sempronius, awed and afraid to ask them their names.

"Long live the City of the Seven Hills!" they answered. "To-morrow the spoils of thirty cities will enrich her shrines!"

Then they slowly mounted their steeds and rode a little way onward until they came to the door of Vesta's temple. There a whirlwind seemed suddenly to arise, a cloud of dust filled the air, and the white horses and their white riders were hidden from sight, and no man ever saw them again.

The next day, Aulus, the dictator, at the head of his army, returned to Rome, bringing with him, as the strangers had foretold, the spoils of thirty cities. But when the people would have lauded him for his victory he would not permit it.

"It is not to me that the honor is due," he said, "but to two white strangers who brought us timely aid and joined most valiantly in the fray. For, indeed, the day was going hard against us and the Latins were crowding upon us on every side, when, looking up, I was surprised to see two strange warriors of princely mien riding beside me. Never in my life saw I twins so much alike. Their armor was white as snow, as were also the two war-horses which they bestrode; and their appearance was such that not all the hosts of our enemies could have thrown so great a spell of fear upon me. But I saw at once that they were our friends, for, couching their spears and laying on about them, they rode into the ranks of the foe, and all the thirty armies were filled with dread. Then our foemen wavered; they fell back; they were routed; and, following in the lead of the two white strangers, our men pursued them right and left, and paused not until the victory was assured. But when we looked around for the princely pair that had led us so valiantly, they were nowhere to be found; they had vanished as suddenly as they had come among us. It is to them that all honor is due for saving Rome, and did

I but know their names they should not want for a fitting monument."

Then Sergius, the pontiff, rose and spoke:

"Romans," said he, "the gods have been with us, and it is they who have saved our city and our homes. These white strangers are the great twin brethren, Castor and Pollux, and the white horses which they rode are the immortal steeds Cyllarus and Harpagus; and we shall be wanting in gratitude if we fail to give them due honor."

Thereupon the dictator, Aulus Postumius Albinus, vowed to build a temple to the Great Twin Brethren, on that spot where they paused to wash their steeds—and there, as you see, it stands today. And every year, on the ides of Quintilis, the Roman equites, mounted on their best horses, ride in procession through the streets to the door of the temple, and all the people delight in honoring the memory of Castor and Pollux and their two gallant steeds, Cyllarus and Harpagus.

THE DANCING HORSES OF SYBARIS

IN the south of Italy there was once a flourishing Greek colony called Sybaris. The town was well situated for commerce, the surrounding country was very fertile, the climate was the finest in the world, and for some centuries the Sybarites were industrious and enterprising, carrying on a profitable trade with other countries, and heaping up immense wealth. But too much good fortune finally proved their ruin. Little by little they lost their habits of labor and thrift, and, instead, gave themselves up to pleasure. Finally, leaving all kinds of necessary work to their slaves, they laid aside the cares of life and spent their days in eating and drinking, in dancing and in listening to fine music, or in attending the circus and watching the feats of acrobats and performing animals.

It is said, indeed, that prizes were offered to any man who would invent some new kind of amusement. A certain flute-player hit upon the idea of teaching the horses to dance, and, since those creatures were as fond as their masters of pleasure, he found it a very easy thing to do. It was not long before the sound of a pipe would set the heels of every war-horse in the country to beating time with it. Imagine, if you please, a whole nation of dancing people and dancing horses—what a free-from-care time of it they must have had!

But the pleasantest summer must come to an end, even

"A CERTAIN FLUTE-PLAYER HIT UPON THE IDEA OF TEACHING THE HORSES TO DANCE"

for grasshoppers. The Sybarites had for neighbors a community of hard workers, students, and tradesmen, called Crotoniates, who lived temperately, drank water from the original Croton River, listened to lectures by Pythagoras, and looked with longing eyes upon the fair gardens and stately white palaces of Sybaris. The Crotoniates several times came to blows with the Sybarites; but as their army was much smaller, and they had no cavalry whatever, they were beaten in every battle. Their foot-soldiers were of no use at all when opposed to the onsets of the Sybarite war-horses.

But true worth is sure to win in the end. When a spy reported to the Crotoniates that he had seen all the horses in Sybaris dancing to the music of a pipe, the Crotoniate general saw his opportunity at once. He sent into the Sybarite territories a company of shepherds and fifers armed with nothing but flutes and shepherd's pipes, while a little way behind them marched the rank and file of the Crotoniate army. When the Sybarites heard that the enemy's forces were coming, they marshaled their cavalry—the finest in the world at that time—and sallied forth to meet them.

They thought it would be fine sport to send the Crotoniates scampering back across the fields into their own country, and half of Sybaris went out to see the fun. What an odd sight it must have been—a thousand fancifully dressed horsemen, splendidly mounted, riding out to meet an array of unarmed shepherds and a handful of ragged foot-soldiers!

The Sybarite ladies wave their handkerchiefs and cheer their champions to the charge. The horsemen sit proudly in their saddles, ready at a word to make the grand dash—

when, hark! a thousand pipes begin to play, not "Yankee Doodle" nor "Rule Britannia," but the national air of Crotona, whatever that may be. The order is given to charge; the Sybarites shout and drive their spurs into their horses' flanks—what fine sport it is going to be! But the war steeds hear nothing, care for nothing, but the music. They lift their slender hoofs in unison with the inspiring strains.

And now the armed Crotoniates appear on the field, but the pipers still pipe, and the horses still dance—they caper, curvet, caracole, pirouette, waltz, trip the light fantastic hoof, forgetful of everything but the delightful harmony. The Sybarite riders have been so sure of the victory that they have taken more trouble to ornament than to arm themselves. Some of them are pulled from their dancing horses by the Crotoniate footmen, others slip to the ground and run as fast as their nerveless legs will carry them back to the shelter of the city walls. The shepherds and fifers retreat slowly toward Crotona, still piping merrily, and the sprightly horses follow them, keeping step with the music.

The dancing horses cross the boundary lines between the two countries, they waltz over the Crotoniate fields, they caracole gaily through the Crotoniate gates, and when the fifers cease their playing the streets of Crotona are full of fine war-horses!

Thus it was that the Sybarites lost the fine cavalry of which they had been so proud. The complete overthrow of their power and the conquest of their city by the Crotoniates followed soon afterward—for how, in any contest against so idle a community, could it have been otherwise?

BUCEPHALUS

OLD Philonicus of Thessaly was the most famous horse-raiser of his time. His stables were talked about from the Adriatic Sea to the Persian Gulf, and many of the best war steeds in Greece and Asia Minor had been bred and partially trained by him. He prided himself particularly on his "ox-headed" horses—broad-browed fellows, with large polls and small, sharp ears, set far apart. Proud creatures these were, and strong, and knowing, and high-spirited—just the kind for war steeds; and that was about all that horses were valued for in those days.

Among these "ox-heads" there was one which excelled all others in mettle, beauty, and size, but which, nevertheless, was a source of great concern to his master. He seemed to be altogether untamable, and, although he was now fourteen years old, there was not a horseman in Greece who had ever been able to mount him. He was a handsome creature—coal-black, with a white star in his forehead. One eye was gray and the other brown. Everybody admired him, and people came great distances to see him. Had Philonicus been less shrewd, he would have sold him for half the price of a common steed, and been glad that he was rid of him. But, like most men who spend their lives among horses, he knew a thing or two. He kept the horse's untamableness a secret, and was careful that only his good points should be exhibited. Everybody who had any use for such an animal wanted to buy him.

"What is the price?"

"Thirteen thousand dollars."

That answer usually put an end to the talk. For, as an ordinary horse might be bought at that time for about seventy dollars, and a thoroughbred war steed for two hundred, who was going to pay such a fabulous price? Half a dozen fine houses could be built for that money. There were rich men who made Philonicus some very handsome offers—a thousand dollars, five thousand, eight thousand—but he held steadily to his first price, and the longer he held to it the more anxious everybody became to buy.

At last, however, after the horse had reached middle age, shrewd Philonicus got his price. King Philip of Macedon, who was ambitious to become the first man of Greece, was the purchaser; and Philonicus, after hearing the gold pieces jingle in his strong-box, led the great Bucephalus up to the Macedonian capital and left him safely housed in the king's stalls. He was careful, no doubt, to get back into his own country before Philip had had time to give the steed any kind of examination.

You may imagine what followed. When the horse was brought out upon the parade ground for trial the skilfullest riders in Macedon could not mount him. He reared and plunged, and beat madly around with his sharp hoofs, until everybody was glad to get safely out of his reach. The greatest horse-tamers of the country were called, but they could do nothing.

"Take him away!" cried the king, at last, in great rage. "That man Philonicus has sold me an utterly wild and unbroken beast, under pretense of his being the finest horse in the world; but he shall rue it."

But now Bucephalus would not be led away. The horse-tamers tried to throw ropes over his feet; they beat him with long poles; they pelted him with stones.

"What a shame to spoil so fine a horse! The awkward cowards know nothing about handling him!" cried the king's son, Alexander, who was standing by.

"Are you finding fault with men who are wiser than yourself?" asked the king, growing still more angry. "Do you, a boy twelve years old, pretend to know more about handling horses than these men, whose business it is?"

"I can certainly handle this horse better," said the prince.

"Suppose you try it!"

"I wish that I might."

"How much will you forfeit if you try, and fail?"

"I will forfeit the price which you paid for the horse," answered Alexander.

Everybody laughed, but the king said, "Stand away, and let the lad try his skill."

Alexander ran quickly to the horse and turned his head toward the sun, for he had noticed that the animal was afraid of his own shadow. Then he spoke softly and gently to him, and kindly stroked his neck. The horse seemed to know that he had found a friend, and little by little his uneasiness left him. Soon with a light spring the lad leaped nimbly upon his back, and without pulling the reins too hard, allowed him to start off at his own gait; and then, when he saw that the horse was no longer afraid, but only proud of his speed, he urged him with voice and spur to do his utmost. The king and his attendants were alarmed, and expected every moment to see the boy unseated and dashed to the ground. But when he turned and rode back, proud of his

The taming of Bucehpalus.

daring feat, everybody cheered and shouted—everybody but his father, who wept for joy and, kissing him, said:

"You must look for a kingdom which is worthy of you, my son, for Macedonia is too small for you."

After that, Bucephalus would allow his groom to mount him barebacked; but when he was saddled nobody but Alexander dared touch him. He would even kneel to his young master, in order that he might mount more easily; and for sixteen years thereafter he served him as faithfully as horse ever served man. Of course, he was with Alexander when he conquered Persia, and he carried him into more than one hard-fought battle. At one time (I think it was in Hyrcania) he was stolen; but his master made proclamation that unless he were forthcoming within a certain time, every man, woman, and child in the province should be put to death, and it was not long before he was brought back.

In the great battle that was fought with King Porus, of India, Alexander recklessly rode too far into the enemy's ranks. The horse and his rider became the target for every spear, and for a time it seemed as if neither could escape. But the gallant Bucephalus, pierced by many weapons, and with streams of blood flowing from his neck and sides, turned about and, overriding the foes which beset them, rushed back to a place of safety. When he saw that his master was out of danger and among friends, the horse sank down upon the grass and died. Historians say that this happened in the year 327 b.c., and that Bucephalus had reached the good old age—for a horse—of thirty years. Alexander mourned for him as for his dearest friend, and the next city which he founded he named Bucephalia, in honor of the steed that had served him so well.

RAKUSH AND HIS MASTER

I. THE PRINCE

RUSTEM was eight years old when his grandfather, the mightiest of all the princes of Iran, came up out of Seistan to see him. For the old man had heard that the boy excelled all others in stature and beauty, and the fame of his strength was known throughout the whole of Persia. At the head, therefore, of a splendid retinue of warriors, the aged prince set out for Zaboulistan, the home of Rustem and his noble father, the white-headed Zal. When he was yet a day's journey from the city, the young boy, mounted on an elephant of war and accompanied by a cavalcade of lords and nobles, went out to meet him.

As the long line of riders wound through the defiles of the mountains or passed in orderly array across the plains, it presented a picture of splendor and beauty which, even in the gorgeous East, has seldom been surpassed. The young prince's body-guard, mounted on coal-black steeds, rode in advance. They were armed with golden maces and with battle-axes that gleamed like silver, and they carried the red banner of the house of Zal. Then followed the elephants, upon whose backs were the nobility of Zaboulistan, seated in howdahs decked with curtains of embroidered silk and ornamented with flags and waving plumes. After these came a thousand young men, the flower of the land of

Iran, riding on horseback, with swords at their sides and long spears resting upon their saddle-bows. The march, moreover, was enlivened with music and song, and nothing was left undone that would give pleasure to the boy or add to the sincerity of the welcome which was to be accorded to the ruler of Seistan.

When at length Rustem saw his grandfather's caravan a long way off, he bade his own retinue stand still, while he, dismounting from his elephant, went forward on foot. And when he drew near and could look into the face of the old prince, he bowed his head to the ground, and cried out, "O mighty ruler of Seistan, and prince of princes in Iran, I am Rustem, thy grandchild! Give me, I pray thee, thy blessing, ere I return to my father's house."

The aged man was astonished, for he saw that not the half had been told him concerning the boy's stature and grace. He commanded his elephant to kneel while he descended and lifted him up and blessed him, and placed him in the howdah beside him; and the two rode side by side into Zaboulistan.

"For more than a hundred years," said the grandfather, "have I been the chief of the princes of Iran, and at no time has anyone arisen to dispute my will. Yet never have my eyes been gladdened as now. I am an old, old man, and you are only a child; but you shall soon sit on my throne and enjoy the pleasures which have been mine, and wield the power both in your father's kingdom and in my own."

"I am glad," answered Rustem, "that I can call you my grandfather. But I care nothing at all for pleasure, and I never think of play, or rest, or sleep. What I want most of all things is a horse of my own, and a hard saddle such as the Turanian riders use, and a coat-of-mail and a helmet like those your warriors have. Then with my lance and my arrows, which I already can use quite well, I will vanquish the enemies of Iran, and my courage shall be like yours and my father's."

This speech pleased the old prince very much, and he blessed Rustem again, and promised him that as soon as he should reach the ordinary stature of a man he should have his wish. During the whole of his stay in Zaboulistan he wanted the boy to be always with him, nor did he care to see anyone else. And when, at the end of the month, messengers came from Seistan with news which obliged him to return, he said to his son, the white-headed Zal: "Remember, that when this child's stature is equal to thine he shall have a horse of his own choosing, a hard saddle like that of a Turanian rider, and a coat-of-mail and a helmet such as we ourselves wear into battle. And forget not this—my last command."

"And see, father," said Rustem, "am I not now almost as tall as you?"

Zal smiled and promised that he would remember.

But before Rustem reached the stature of his father, the good prince of Seistan had passed from the earth, and Zal, himself an old man, had succeeded to his throne. Then news was brought that a vast army of Turanians, the foes of Iran, had come down from the north and were threatening to cross into Persia. They had even cut in pieces an army which the Shah had sent out against them, and messengers had arrived in Zaboulistan beseeching aid from Zal. Then Rustem begged of his father that he might lead a band of young men against the invaders.

"It is true," said he, "that I am only a child in years. But, although I am not quite so tall as you, my stature is now equal to that of ordinary men; and I am skilled in the use of all kinds of weapons. Give me therefore the steed that was promised me, and the mace of my grandfather, and let me go to the succor of Iran."

These words pleased Zal not a little, and he answered: "O my son, thou art still very young, and thy lips smell of milk, and thy days should be given to play. But the times are full of danger, and Iran must look to thee for help."

Then he at once sent out a proclamation into all the Persian provinces, commanding that on the first day of the approaching Festival of Roses all the choicest horses, of whatsoever breed, should be brought to Zaboulistan in order that Rustem might select from among them his steed of battle. For the one that was chosen, its owner should receive mountains of gold in exchange; but should any man conceal a steed of value, or fail to bring it for the prince's inspection, he should be punished without mercy.

II. THE STEED

ON the day appointed, the finest horses in all Persia were assembled at Zaboulistan. The most famous breeders from Kabul and the Afghan pasture-lands were there with their choicest stock, and the hill-slopes to the south of the city were white with tents. A caravan of low-browed men from the shores of the Caspian had just arrived, weary with their journey, but proud of their horsemanship and of the clean-limbed, swiftly moving animals which they had brought fresh from the freedom of the steppes, and which they were accustomed to ride at full speed, while standing erect on their saddles. Near them were the tents of a patriarchal sheik, who had come from the distant valley of the Euphrates, bringing his numerous family and his large following of servants and herdsmen, and four matchless Arab coursers, for which he had already refused more than one princely offer. But the greater number of horses had been brought in by the men of Seistan, some of whom were encamped outside the walls, while others lodged with friends and acquaintances in the city. Most of these last had brought only a single animal each, and they had done this not so much for the hope of reward, as for the fear of punishment. Every one had brought the best that he had, and I doubt if the world has ever seen a nobler or more wonderful collection of steeds.

At an early hour in the morning, the whole city was astir. Everybody, both within and without the walls, was moving toward the western gate, just outside of which Prince Zal and young Rustem had already taken their stand, in order to inspect the animals that would be presented. A troop of armed men was drawn up in such a way as to form a passage through which the competing horses were to be led directly in front of Rustem. On the top of the wall was a covered pavilion, from which the ladies of Zaboulistan, without being seen, could look down upon the concourse below.

At a given signal, the horses, which had already been brought together at a convenient spot, were led, one by one, before the prince. The first were those of the Zaboulistan herds—strong, beautiful steeds, many of which had been bred and cared for with the sole thought of their being chosen for the use of Rustem.

"FRESH FROM THE FREEDOM OF THE STEPPES."

"Do you desire swiftness?" asked the keeper of the foremost. "Here is a steed that can outstrip the wind."

"Not swiftness only, but strength," answered Rustem. Then he placed his hand upon the horse to see if it could stand that test; and the animal shuddered beneath his grasp and sank upon its haunches from the strength of the pressure. Thus it fared with all the steeds that were brought forward.

"Do you want a perfect steed?" asked the long-bearded sheik from the west. "If so, here are beauty and strength and swiftness and intelligence, all combined in one." And he led forward the largest of his Arabs.

There was a murmur of admiration from all the lookers-on, for seldom, in that land of beautiful horses, had an animal been seen which was in every way so perfect. Rustem said nothing, but quietly subjected the steed to the same test that he had applied to the others. Lastly, the traders from Kabul brought forward a herd of ten which they had carefully selected as the strongest from among all that had been bred in the Afghan pastures. But every one of them quailed beneath Rustem's iron hand.

"Whose is that mare that feeds on the plain beyond your tents?" asked Rustem. "And whose is the colt that follows after her? I see no marks on its flanks."

"We do not know," answered the men from Kabul. "But they have followed us all the way from the Afghan valleys, and we have been unable either to drive them back or to capture them. We have heard it said, however, that men call the colt Rakush, or Lightning, and that, although it has now been three years ready for the saddle, its mother defends it and will let no one touch it."

The colt was a beautiful animal. Its color was that of rose-leaves scattered upon a saffron ground, its chest and shoulders were like those of a lion, and its eyes beamed with the fire of intelligence. Snatching a lariat from the hands of a herdsman, Rustem ran quickly forward and threw the noose over the animal's head. Then followed a terrible battle, not so much with the colt as with its mother. But in the end Rustem was the winner, and the mare retired crestfallen from the field. With a great bound the young prince leaped upon Rakush's back, and the rose-colored steed bore him over the plains with the speed of the wind. But when the animal had become thoroughly tired, he turned at a word from his master and went back to the city gate.

"This is the horse that I choose," said Rustem to his father. "Let us give to the Afghan herdsmen the prize that is due."

"Nay," answered the herdsmen; "if thou be Rustem, take him and save Iran from its foes. For his price is the land of Iran, and, seated upon him, no enemy can stand before thee."

And that is the way in which Rustem won his war steed.

III. THE DRAGON

TO relate all the adventures of Rakush and his master,— how they led the men of Iran against the Turanians, how they alone put whole armies to flight, how they vanquished the Deevs in their mountain-fastnesses, and how they extended the dominions of the Shah from the sea to the great salt plains,—would alone fill a volume. Their names were known throughout the length and breadth of Iran, and so inseparable were they that one was never mentioned save in connection with the other. It will be enough if I relate a single one of their adventures.

It chanced upon a time that the great Shah conceived the foolish plan of conquering Mazinderan and obliging the king of that country to pay him tribute. But the small army which he led was utterly defeated by the forces of Mazinderan, and he himself, being taken prisoner, was thrown into a dungeon where the light of day was never seen. Nevertheless, with the aid of one of his keepers, he contrived to write and send a letter to Prince Zal of Zaboulistan. After narrating all his misfortunes, he said:

"I have sought what the foolish seek, and I have found what the foolish find. And if thou wilt not speedily send me help I shall surely perish."

When Zal received this letter he was much troubled, and he gnawed his very finger-tips for vexation. For the Shah's expedition had been undertaken contrary to his advice. Yet he called to Rustem and said: "See how our lord the Shah has been vanquished by his enemies. It has happened just as I told him, and yet it behooves us to send him aid. Saddle Rakush, therefore, and cast your leopard-skin about you, and hasten by the nearest route to the deliverance of Iran's ruler."

"It is well, my father," said Rustem. "My sword is ready, and I will ride alone into Mazinderan. And if fortune favor me I will retrieve the losses that have been suffered there."

Then he mounted Rakush and set out by the shortest road across the Great Salt Desert that lies toward Mazinderan; and such was the speed of the good horse that in twelve hours they accomplished a journey of more than two days. Late in the evening Rustem dismounted, and having taken the saddle from the horse's back, he turned him loose to graze upon the scant herbage. Then he built a fire of dry brush and lay down beside it to rest for the night.

A fierce lion, who had his lair in a cluster of reeds close by, saw the tall man and the rose-colored steed, and crept forward to attack them. Rakush heard him coming and hastened to meet him; and before the lion could make a spring, the horse leaped upon him and beat him down with his hoofs and stamped upon him till he died. Rustem, awakened by the great noise, sprang to his feet only in time to see the dead lion upon the ground, and the horse still trampling upon him. He was angry that Rakush, instead of himself, had slain the beast, and instead of praising the faithful animal he scolded him unmercifully.

"O rash and foolish steed!" he cried, "who told you to fight with lions? You should have awakened me at the first, for had you been killed in your folly, who would have carried me into Mazinderan?"

Then he lay down again to sleep; but the horse was much grieved by his unkind words.

At the first peep of dawn Rustem was again in the saddle. All day long he rode over the barren wastes where there was no green thing nor anywhere a drop of water. The hot sun beat pitilessly down upon man and horse, and the sand beneath them was like a burning oven. At length Rustem was so overcome by the heat and with thirst that he lost all hope, and alighting from his steed lay down in the sand to die. But while he was commending his soul to God and expecting that every moment would be the last, he chanced to see a fine sheep running at no great distance.

"Surely," thought he, "there must be water not far away, or this animal could not be here."

The hope gave him new courage, and remounting Rakush, he urged him forward in pursuit of the sheep. Nor did they have to follow it far, for it led them into a narrow green valley, through the middle of which ran a little brook. And man and beast drank their fill, and while Rustem gave thanks to Ormuzd for their deliverance, Rakush nipped the fresh herbage that grew along the banks of the stream. When at length the sun had set and the stars had risen, Rustem lay down to sleep. But first he charged his steed that he should not fight with any wild beasts.

"If any danger come," said he, "you must waken me at once, and I will defend both myself and you."

Rakush listened to his master's words, and then returned quietly to his grazing. All went well until near midnight, when a fierce dragon which lived in that valley, coming out of his den, was astonished to see the horse feeding and a man asleep not far away. Angry that anyone should intrude upon his domain, he was just ready to rush upon them and destroy them with his poisonous breath, when Rakush, seeing the danger, hastened to awaken his master. At the sound of the horse's shrill neighing, Rustem sprang up quickly and seized his sword, expecting to meet an enemy. But the wily dragon had hastened back into his den, and no cause of fear could be seen in all the valley.

"Unkind steed that you are," cried Rustem, angrily, "why do you thus needlessly disturb my sleep? "

Then he lay down again to rest. Soon the dragon came out a second time, fiercer than before, and a second time did Rakush waken his master in vain. A third time did this happen, and a fourth, and then Rustem could no longer restrain his anger. He heaped reproaches, upon the horse and abused him with vile epithets, and declared that if his slumbers were again disturbed thus uselessly, he would kill him and make his way on foot into Mazinderan.

Rakush, although distressed, was as watchful as before. When the dragon came out the fifth time he hastened quickly to waken his master. Rustem, filled with rage, sprang up and seized his sword, intending to slay his best friend. But this time he saw the dragon ere it could return to its den, and there followed such a battle as had never been seen before. The dragon leaped upon Rustem and wrapped itself about him, and would surely have crushed him to death had not Rakush come to the rescue. With his teeth the horse seized the reptile from behind, and as it turned to defend itself, Rustem's arm was freed so that he could use his sword. With one mighty stroke he cut off the dragon's head; and the vile pest of the desert was no more.

Then Rustem praised Rakush for his valor, and washed him in the stream, and fondled him until the break of day; and the horse forgot the unkind words that had been spoken to him. And when the sun arose they set out on another day's journey across the burning sands.

But I need not follow them farther on their perilous way, nor relate what befell them in the land of the magicians and in the country of darkness, where there was no light of sun or stars, and where they were guided by Rakush's instinct alone. Neither will I tell of their adventures after they had come into Mazinderan, nor how, after meeting innumerable dangers, they delivered the Shah from his dungeon, and rallied his scattered army and led it to victory. These things are narrated in the songs of Firdusi, the Persian poet.

IV. THE PITFALL

NEVER in all the East was there a hero that could be likened unto Rustem, and never a horse that could in any way be compared with Rakush. Many years passed by,— years of peace and years of war,—and many Shahs sat upon the throne of Iran, but the real power was in the hands of Rustem of Zaboulistan. And although he lived to a great age, and Rakush was so very, very old that he was no longer of the color of rose-leaves, but white as the snow of winter, yet both of them retained their strength and their wisdom to the end. And the end came in this way:

The king of Kabul had become tired of paying tribute to Rustem, and he resolved, if possible, to bring about the old hero's death, and thus free himself from that burden. Hence, by the advice of his nobles, he invited Rustem to visit him in his country palace, where they could spend the summer months in hunting and in other amusements, of which both were very fond. Rustem suspected no guile, for he had enjoyed the king's hospitality many times before. He therefore accepted the invitation, and with Rakush and a retinue of his noblest men, arrived in due time at the king's summer home. The king had prepared a royal welcome for him, and for several days they feasted together and made merry in the palace. Then a great hunt in the forest was proposed, and to this Rustem gladly consented, because, next to feats of courage in battle, he loved the excitement of the chase.

It was known that there were many wild animals in the mountain valleys, and the company set out from the palace with high expectations—for but few of the guests suspected the dark designs of the king. All went well until the afternoon, and much game of all kinds was taken. At length a deer was started from its covert, and all the party gave chase. But Rustem, through the king's designing, followed a different pathway from that taken by the others—a pathway across which deep pits had been dug and then carefully concealed with leaves and sod. Huntsmen had been stationed here and there to direct Rustem into the snare, and he rode fearlessly onward, looking for nothing except traces of the fleeing deer.

When they came to the first pit, Rakush smelled the newly turned soil and stopped suddenly. Rustem urged him to go forward, but the horse, for the first time in his long life, refused to obey. Then Rustem, growing impatient, urged him still harder, but he reared upon his hind feet and tried to turn back. This aroused Rustem's anger, and, raising his whip, he struck the faithful beast—a thing that until this sad day had never been done. So grieved and terrified was Rakush that he sprang forward and fell into the pit, and both horse and rider were pierced with the sharp spears which projected, points upward, from the bottom.

As they lay weltering in their blood and dying, the king of Kabul came up, and seeing their plight, pretended to be overcome with grief.

"O matchless hero," he cried to Rustem, "what mishap is this that has befallen thee? I will run and call my physicians to come to thy aid."

But Rustem answered: "Thou traitor, this is thy doing. The time for physicians is past, and there is for me no healing save that of death, which comes once to all men! I pray thee, however, to place beside me my bow and two arrows, and deny not this my last request. For I would not that while thou art calling a physician, a lion should come upon me and devour me."

Without taking thought, the king did as Rustem desired; but he had no sooner placed the bow within the hero's reach than, filled with fear, he ran and hid himself in a hollow tree which stood close by.

Rustem, in great agony, raised the bow, and with his last strength shot an arrow with such force that it transfixed the king where he stood and pinned him to the tree. Then the hero gave thanks to Ormuzd the Good, that he had been permitted thus to take vengeance upon the traitor. And when he had spoken he fell back upon his horse, and Rakush and his master, in the same moment, passed from the world.

BROIEFORT, THE BLACK ARABIAN

I. THE GIFT OF FORTUNE

"I WOULD rather have that horse than aught else that now is or ever has been."

It must have been a rare animal indeed to bring this exclamation from the mouth of young Ogier the Dane, while he was fighting a hand-to-hand duel with Brunamont, the giant king and champion of the Moors. He knew that his life depended upon the issue of that fight, and yet he could not think of anything but his enemy's steed; and, as he stood thrusting and parrying with his sword, he kept repeating to himself:

"Ah! if Fortune and the good angels would only give me that horse!"

And at last Fortune did favor him. Fierce Brunamont was overthrown and left senseless upon the field, the Moorish host was routed with great slaughter, and Ogier secured the steed which he had coveted so much. And when he mounted the handsome creature and rode between the tents where flew the banners of Charlemagne, there was not a prouder man in all Europe than he. His fellow warriors cheered him for the gallant victory which he had helped to win; but his mind was all on the horse. He kept patting the animal on the neck and saying over and over again:

"Now thanks to fairy Fortune, that has given me this

steed, whom I wished for more than anything else in the broad world! So long as I live there shall nothing persuade me to part with my good Broiefort—the war-horse whom Fortune allowed me to win fairly at the risk of my life."

It was a matter of common talk,—and therefore true,—that Broiefort had been reared in Arabia, whence all the best horses come. Save for his forehead, in which there was a snow-white new moon, and his two fore feet, which were also white, he was the color of polished ebony. He was very strong, and his arching neck and slender legs and shapely head were admired by everybody that saw him. He was teachable, gentle, wise, and brave, and it was not long until he loved Ogier as well as Ogier loved him. For many years after the famous battle with Brunamont, the flaxen-haired Dane and the black Arabian were never separated for a day, and people remarked that it was as rare to see Ogier without Broiefort as to see a sword without its hilt.

There came a time, however, after both were beginning to grow old, that there was a turn in the tide of their good fortune. An accident, which had happened through no fault of Ogier's, had caused Charlemagne to become his enemy. The faithful old warrior was banished from France, and all the rich estates which had been his were forfeited. He had no longer a penny, nor even so much land as he could lie down upon. But why should he despair? He still had Broiefort. On the good horse's back he would ride out of France and seek a home and fortune among strangers. He rode over the Alps into Italy and told his story to Didier, the king of the Lombards. Didier was glad to welcome so famous a warrior: he would make him one of the foremost men in his kingdom. And so Ogier put his hands into the hands of the Lombard king and did him homage, and received in return the command of two castles on the river Rhone.

II. THE BATTLE

BUT Charlemagne would not allow his former friend and warrior-chief to rest in peace, even in the domains of the Lombard king. No sooner did he hear that Didier had befriended the exiled Dane than he sent a messenger into Lombardy, demanding that Ogier should be returned to France, chained like a greyhound.

"Never will I do so base a thing!" cried Didier. "Sooner than desert the friend who has sworn fealty to me, I will see all Lombardy overrun by my foes, my own palace in ashes, and myself laid low with the thrusts of Charlemagne's spears!"

The messenger returned to France with this answer, and Didier and Ogier made ready for war; for well they knew that Charlemagne was not a man to be trifled with.

Early the next spring a mighty army, led by Charlemagne himself, crossed the Alps for the purpose of overrunning Lombardy and capturing the exiled Dane. A bloody battle was fought on the plains of St. Ajossa—such a battle as neither Lombard nor Frank had ever seen before. For hours the conflict raged; and everywhere Ogier and the steed Broiefort were in the thickest of the fray. Never did man and horse fight more bravely. The old knight's shield was pierced in thirty places, his helmet was split in twain, he was wounded with seven spears; and yet, even after he knew that the day was lost, he kept on fighting like a tiger.

At last Ogier is unhorsed. Broiefort, maddened for the

"EVERYWHERE OGIER AND HIS STEED WERE
IN THE THICKEST OF THE FRAY.

moment, flees across the field, pursued by a hundred soldiers. Flinging right and left with his heels, he kills three
squires and five horses, and puts a whole company of
Frenchmen to flight. Not a weapon can be made to touch
him. Men say that he has a charmed life. Coming to the
top of a little knoll, he turns his head and looks back. He
sees his master in the midst of the mêlée, surrounded by
enemies, with one knee on the ground, fighting a losing
fight. Shall he desert his friend in his greatest need?

He wheels about and returns to the field, scattering his
three hundred pursuers before him. Ogier has begun to
lose hope. His sword is broken. The Frenchmen are closing upon him. Suddenly he hears a neigh, and looking up
he sees Broiefort pressing toward him through the crowd.
In another moment he has swung himself into the saddle,
and knight and steed are flying over the plain with—as
truthful old stories tell us—fifteen thousand men in hot
pursuit. But who can overtake Broiefort?

III. THE FLIGHT

LATE in the evening, Ogier, wearied with the long ride
and overcome by the pain of his wounds, thought that it
would be safe for him to stop and rest. He dismounted near
a spring of water which gurgled out from beneath a huge
rock, and, after slaking his thirst, he bathed his hot head
in the stream, and washed the smoking sides and mud-
bespattered legs of his steed. Then, sitting on the ground
with his back resting against the rock, he soon fell asleep;
but Broiefort stood by him to watch.

Half an hour passed quietly, and then a faint sound was
heard far down the road. The horse pricked up his ears

and listened. Very soon he could distinguish quite plainly the thump, thump of galloping hoofs coming closer every moment, and he knew that it meant danger. He whinnied to awaken his master; but Ogier slept on. He came closer to him, and stamped his feet against the rock; Ogier stirred a little, but did not waken. Then he stamped still harder, and neighed shrilly three times; but his master, dreaming of battle, did not hear him. By this time their pursuers were in sight. Ten men—yes, a thousand men—with lances poised and swords drawn, ready to fall upon Ogier wherever they might find him. were coming pell-mell along the highway!

Broiefort was desperate. He seized his master by the collar, and lifting him to his feet shook him roughly. Ogier awoke just in time. He vaulted quickly into the saddle, while the lances of his foremost pursuers almost grazed his armor. His faithful steed leaped forward, and in a few moments he was safely out of reach and out of hearing again.

For three whole days Broiefort carried his master through mountain passes and forests, so closely pressed that there was no time to stop anywhere for food or rest. For three months the chase was kept up, although the pursuers now and then lost track of the fugitives long enough to allow Ogier to rest a night in some out-of-the-way castle, where Broiefort was sure to be regaled with a measure of oats. At last, after many adventures, they reached one of Ogier's old strongholds on the river Rhone, where—according to the historian—they were besieged by Charlemagne with an army of ten thousand warriors.

IV. THE SIEGE

THERE were only three hundred men—vassals of Ogier—in the castle, but the most of them were known to be good and true, and the Dane felt that, for a time at least, he was safe from any harm that the besiegers could do him. Broiefort was given a warm stall, with plenty of straw, in the cellar, and as there was a great stole of provisions in the castle, the inmates were all as comfortable as need be. Ogier knew that no power on earth could batter down the walls of the castle, for they were of Saracen work,—that is, the mortar had been boiled in blood,—and hence they were proof against every kind of weapon. All that the garrison had to do, therefore, was to prevent the besiegers from putting up scaling-ladders, and this required only a little watchfulness.

At length, however, Charlemagne caused a wooden tower to be built in front of the gate—a tower seven stories high, on which a thousand knights and a hundred and seventy archers could stand, and from which they hurled missiles and shot countless arrows over the castle wall. Then, indeed, sad days began for Ogier. One by one his men were picked off the walls by the sharpshooters in the high tower; one by one his squires and the faithfullest defenders of the castle met their death. Finally, there was no one left alive but himself and the horse Broiefort—two besieged by ten thousand. But they had held out well; for, according to the old song-writers, it was now seven years since Charlemagne had begun the siege.

And now Ogier bethought him that if he could escape to his native country, Denmark, his own kinsfolk might befriend and shelter him. The chance was worthy of a trial, at least. Very early one morning, therefore, he went down to visit Broiefort in his stall. There was not another handful of oats in the castle; not a grain of corn, not a wisp of hay was to be found. Ogier himself had not had a mouthful of food for two days. To hold the place longer was to starve.

"Horse," said Ogier, stroking the creature's neck and sides,—"horse, so good and brave and proud! You have stood by me well. A firm friend you have been in many a strait. I wonder if you will help me once again?"

Broiefort understood every word; he whinnied softly in reply; he struck his foot upon the stone pavement as if to say that he was ready to be going. Ogier brought out his saddle, now so long unused, and the bridle with the golden bits. Broiefort leaped into the air for very gladness. And when his master threw the rich trappings upon his back, tightened the saddle-girths, and laid the reins over his neck, he seemed beside himself with joy. Then Ogier donned his own armor, buckled his good sword to his side, and put his bright steel helmet upon his head. Leading the horse across the courtyard, he opened the castle gate quietly and peeped out. The besiegers were all asleep in their tents; even the sentinels were sprawled upon the ground, dreaming of their homes and their loved ones in faraway Aquitaine.

Ogier let down the drawbridge very softly, and then, mounting Broiefort, he rode out of the fortress which had sheltered him so long. Good Broiefort seemed to understand everything. With eyes open very wide and ears alert to catch every sound, he stepped so lightly that the most wakeful of the besiegers did not hear him. The birds were singing in the tree-tops as they passed through Charlemagne's camp, but not a soldier was stirring. Once safely outside the lines, Broiefort changed his whole manner. Throwing up his head and pointing his ears forward, he broke into a long, steady gallop—a gait which he could keep up all day without tiring. And thus Ogier, safe out of the reach of his foes, rode northward through sunny France.

V. THE CAPTURE

ON the fifth day they had put so many miles between themselves and the besiegers that the great Dane began to feel himself safe. In another day they would cross the Rhine, and then on to Denmark! At about noon they stopped to rest by a spring which bubbled up from the ground near the foot of a rocky hill. Ogier, very tired from his long ride, and thankful that the worst of it was over, lay down upon the grass and soon fell asleep. Broiefort, not thinking that any watch was needed, now that they were so far from their enemies, wandered here and there, nipping the young clover that was just beginning to blossom in the fields.

He was very hungry and the clover was very good, and hence he did not notice a company of priests and knights that came riding down the highway, or, if he noticed them, he did not think of their harming his master. He therefore kept on grazing, and neglected to awaken Ogier and warn him of the possible danger. At the head of the company was the archbishop of Rheims, who had been making his usual rounds among the sick people of the neighborhood, and was returning to his palace. He was himself a warrior of no little note, and therefore delighted always to have a retinue of knights and squires around him. One of these young men, seeing Ogier asleep upon the ground, was so struck by his noble appearance that he rode back quickly and told his master. The archbishop, curious to know who it might be, spurred his horse and, followed by his whole company, cantered down to the spring. The old man was astounded when he saw that it was Ogier, for he had marched with the Dane in many a campaign, and fought by his side in many a hard-won battle.

He would have given a whole year's revenue if he had not seen him, for it pained his heart to think that he was obliged to make a prisoner of his old friend and comrade and deliver him into the hands of the king. But his oath of fealty to Charlemagne would not allow him to do otherwise. At his command, therefore, one of his knights secured Ogier's sword, another his shield, and another the good horse Broiefort. Then twenty men with drawn swords stood around the fugitive while the archbishop awakened him.

"My old-time friend, Ogier," he said, "awake and look around you! You can see that it is useless for you to resist; for here are forty men, most of them armed, while you are unarmed and alone. Yield yourself, then, as our prisoner!"

But Ogier was not the man to be taken so easily. He sprang to his feet, and with a blow of his great fist crushed the head of the knight who stood nearest to him. Then he tore the saddle from the back of one of the priest's pack-horses, and with it dealt furiously about him until ten of his assailants were laid sprawling in the dust, and the rude weapon was broken in pieces in his hands. But the struggle was of no avail, for other knights closing in upon him, he was wounded sorely, and finally bound hand and foot with strong ropes. He begged his captors that they would kill him then and there, rather than give him up to Charlemagne. They made no answer, however, but put him astride of a mule, tied his feet together underneath, and took him into Rheims, where the archbishop ordered him to be placed in his own prison.

As for Broiefort, the gallant horse was taken to Meaux, where he was made to draw a heavy two-wheeled cart loaded with stones and bricks and mortar. For seven years he toiled, half-fed, broken-spirited, hopeless. His once beautiful coat became rough and ragged, showing the outlines of every rib beneath; his mane, unkempt and uncared for, was knotted in many a snarl; his long tail, which had once been his pride, was filled with burs and thorns; his breast and shoulders were galled by the ill-fitting harness; his eyes lost their fire, and his chin drooped with despair.

VI. THE PRISON

FOR seven years, also, Ogier languished in prison. Charlemagne would have been glad to put him to death, but he knew that every knight in France would cry out against it. So long, however, as the good archbishop lived, the brave Dane fared much better than his horse. Every day he was given a gallon of wine to drink, and two loaves of bread and the half of a pig to eat. The ladies and squires and burgesses of Rheims came often to his cell to visit him, and the archbishop played chess with him almost every evening. His beard became white as snow, but his arms remained as big and as strong as ever, and he never lost hope.

By and by, however, sad changes came to France and to Ogier. The archbishop was slain in that famous fight at Roncesvalles, where all the flower of French chivalry perished. The prison at Rheims passed into the hands of other keepers. All of Ogier's old friends were dead, and it was not long until Ogier himself seemed to be forgotten.

Charlemagne was hard beset by his foes. A pagan king named Brehus invaded France from the south, and threatened to overrun the whole empire. Battle after battle was fought, and the French, having no leaders, were beaten every time. Everybody was in despair. People began to compare the former glorious times with the present. They thought of Roland and of Oliver, and of Reinold, and of the brave archbishop of Rheims, who used to lead them in battle—all dead, now. Then they thought of Ogier, and wondered if he, too, was dead.

"If we only had Ogier to lead us!" said some.

And the cry was echoed by many others: "If we only had Ogier to lead us!"

"Ogier is not dead. He is still in the prison at Rheims," said a young knight, a kinsman of the late archbishop. "Let every brave Frenchman petition the king to set him free!"

Thereupon, three hundred knights, all sons of counts, dukes, or princes, marched in a body to Charlemagne's tent, crying: "Ogier! Ogier! Give us Ogier the Dane for our leader!"

The king was angry at first, but seeing that something must be done, he said at last: "I know not whether Ogier be alive or dead. If, however, he be still alive, I will fetch him and make him your leader as you desire."

He sent at once to Rheims to inquire if Ogier were still in prison. Yes, the keeper thought that there was some such man shut up in one of the lower dungeons. The squires who had brought the king's message fancied that they heard him in his dismal cell, fighting the snakes and water-rats which had come into the place from the river. They called to him, and he answered. Then ropes were let down and he was drawn up into the daylight to which he had been for a long time a stranger. He was given a bountiful meal and clad in rich garments, such as he had worn in former days, and then led into the presence of the king.

VII. THE PARDON

CHARLEMAGNE offered to pardon the Dane and to return to him all the vast estates which had once been his, on condition that he would lead the French host against the pagan army under King Brehus. The old hero stood up, as tall and as proud, and seemingly as strong as ever, and answered that if he might wear his own armor and ride the good war steed Broiefort, he would undertake to drive every pagan out of France; otherwise he could not go into battle, but would return to his dungeon and leave the country to its fate.

Ogier's armor was quickly found, but nobody remembered anything about his steed. The king offered his own war-horse to the Dane, but when Ogier leaned his great weight upon it the animal was crushed to the ground. Several other steeds were tried, but all with the same result. Finally, an old priest who had just arrived from Meaux said that he believed that Broiefort himself was still alive, and was used as a draft-horse by the monks of the abbey. Ten squires were sent out at once to bring the old horse to his master.

Ogier wept when he saw the sad plight of his once beautiful war steed, and Broiefort would have done the same had it been possible for horses to weep, so great was his joy. As it was, the fire came back into his eyes; he lifted his head with somewhat of the old-time pride; he scratched his feet with delight; he fondled his master with his jet-black nose, and whinnied softly, as though he wanted to speak. Ogier put his arm over him, and leaned with his whole weight. The horse stood up bravely, and shrank not in the least beneath him. Then the grooms washed the steed in warm spring water, and combed and oiled his mane and tail, and trimmed his fetlocks, and polished his hoofs, and covered him with a richly embroidered cloth, and put the golden bits in his mouth. You would not have known him as the draft-horse that had hauled stones for the abbot of Meaux—he was the Broiefort who fought in the famous battle of St. Ajossa. Brave Ogier wept again, but this time for joy, when he mounted the grand old steed and rode forth to give battle to the pagan invaders.

There is no need to describe that last fierce fight which ended in a hand-to-hand combat between Ogier and King Brehus. In all his lifetime the gallant Dane had never met so equal a foe; and had it not been for Broiefort's aid he would not have come out of the fray alive. The combat was a long one, and the fate of France depended upon the issue. The sun had set, and the twilight was deepening into darkness, and yet neither of the combatants seemed able to gain any advantage over his foe. At last the treacherous pagan, by an overhanded sweep of his long sword, struck Broiefort squarely on the neck. The faithful horse, with a cry of anguish, fell dead to the earth. Never had anything caused Ogier so great grief. But his anger held down his sorrow, and nerved him to desperation. He made one final terrible thrust with his sword, and his pagan foe was stretched lifeless by the side of the steed he loved so well.

Ogier took for his own the gray war-horse, Marchevallé, which King Brehus had ridden in the battle. But nothing could ever console him for the loss of his faithful friend, Broiefort, the matchless black Arabian.

ROZINANTE

HE was never very handsome. Ill-shaped, long-haired, short-maned, big-hoofed, knock-kneed, sway-backed, broad-eared, watery-eyed, slow-paced, awkward—he would hardly have found a buyer at any price, if put up at auction. But in the eyes of his master, Don Quixote, he was the handsomest and the wisest steed that had ever lived.

"Talk as you will about Alexander's Bucephalus, or about the Cid's Babieca," said he, "they were but poor jades compared with my gallant charger. Only see, if you will, what a soft coat he has, what a splendid head, what a Roman nose, and what sound teeth, always ready for action. And then he is the gentlest, knowingest beast that ever bore brave knight into the tournament or the battlefield."

He had been only a common farm horse, used for carrying burdens and drawing the plow, and as such he had never had any name of his own. He was called the nag, or the colt, or simply the horse—for there was no other creature of this kind about the place, and hence there was no need of a more distinctive title. But when his master made up his mind to turn knight-errant and roam through the world in quest of adventures, it became necessary to find some name for him that would be worthy of a steed with so noble a destiny.

Don Quixote spent four whole days in thinking about it. He wanted to give him a high-sounding name—one that would fill your mouth when you spoke it, and impress you with some idea of the greatness of his master. It should also be an expressive name—one that had some meaning to it and would give some hint of the horse's former condition, as well as his present station. It was hard to find such a name. Don Quixote made a list of all the names that he had ever heard about, from Pegasus to Bayard, and from Hector's Galathe to Count Raymond's Aquiline, but none of them was suitable to his own horse. At last, however, a bright thought came into his mind.

"Was he not a common horse before, and is he not now before all common horses? Then what better name can be given him than Rozinante, which means common-horse-before? There is nothing in the world so simple or so easily understood."

And so the troublesome matter was settled, and the steed was called Rozinante. Then his master, having donned some rusty old pieces of armor which had not been worn for a hundred years or more, mounted him and rode out in search of knightly adventures. It was no doubt a funny sight to all who saw them—the lean and sorry horse, ill-fed and ill-kept, and his strangely accoutered rider, wandering through the country to protect the innocent, to punish evil-doers, and to perform brave deeds generally. But to Don Quixote it was the most serious thing possible. "When the history of my famous achievements is given to the world," he said to himself, "the learned author will doubtless begin it in this manner:

" 'Scarce had the ruddy-colored Phœbus begun to spread the golden tresses of his hair over the vast surface of the earthly globe, and scarce had those feathered poets of the grove, the pretty painted birds, tuned their little pipes to sing their early welcomes to the beauteous Aurora, when the renowned knight Don Quixote de la Mancha, disdaining soft repose, forsook the sleep-inviting couch, and mounting his famous steed Rozinante, entered the ancient and celebrated plains of Montiel!' "

And then, as he proceeded on his way, he cried out, "O happy age! O fortunate times! decreed to usher into the world my famous achievements! And thou, venerable sage, wise enchanter, whatever be thy name; thou whom fate has ordained to be the compiler of my history, forget not, I beseech thee, my trusty Rozinante, the eternal companion of all my adventures!"

Thus, confident of the greatness of his mission, he rode bravely out into the world, with lance in hand, ready to combat and overthrow evil wherever he found it. He made some ludicrous mistakes now and then; in fact, his whole undertaking was a ludicrous mistake, for the days of knight-errantry had ended long before his time. But he was as earnest about it all as ever was the bravest hero of old; and of course Rozinante could do nothing but serve him faithfully so far as his strength would allow.

Riding one day with his squire Sancho Panza at his side, the would-be knight saw a number of windmills in the fields before them. To his crazed fancy each one of these mills seemed to be a giant stretching his long white arms toward the sky.

"Ah! how lucky!" he cried. "Now we shall have a combat worthy of our steel, and we'll put an end to the whole cursed race of giants."

"I see no giants," said the squire.

"Then you must be blind!" cried his master. "Look at their white arms reaching out toward us and daring us to the combat!"

"Pardon me, sir," said the squire; "but those are windmills."

But Don Quixote had already struck his heels against Rozinante's sides and was speeding down the hill with couched lance to do battle with his long-armed enemies.

"Stand, cowards!" he cried, as he came within speaking distance of the first windmill. "Stand your ground, and fly not basely from a single knight, who comes to meet you all in deadly combat!"

At that moment the wind arose, and the mill sails began to go around quite rapidly, as if daring the mad knight to attack them. Don Quixote became all the braver at this sign of defiance. He covered himself with his shield, and with his lance in position, urged poor Rozinante to his utmost speed. The windmill stood its ground, however, and received the charge with more composure than the knight had reckoned. The lance, sticking fast in the sail, was wrenched out of his hands and broken into shivers; and rider and horse were struck with such force that they were both sent rolling into the sand a good way off. When Don Quixote found his breath again, and was able to rise, he saw the faithful Rozinante standing quietly by him, somewhat the worse for the stroke which had been given him, but ready for any further adventure that his master might wish to undertake.

"I do believe," said the good knight, rubbing his eyes and looking around him, "I do believe that some wizard has transformed all these giants into windmills so as to take away from me the honor of victory."

Then, mounting Rozinante, he rode thoughtfully away.

SWIFT AND OLD-GOLD

FIRST HEAT—THE WEDDING PRESENTS

ICOULD never quite understand why old King Peleus of the little city of Phthia in Thessaly should have been so great a favorite of the gods. But, say what we will, he knew some things that were well worth knowing. For instance, he knew that the best way to govern men was to give them plenty of work to do; and hence his people of Phthia were such busy bodies that they were everywhere called Myrmidons, which in plain English means Ants. Indeed, an absurd story was told that when Peleus first came into that part of the country there was no city there, and not a sign of human beings, not even a wild man in the woods— nothing but a great ant-hill with its thousands of six-legged workers toiling and fuming and laying up their stores of winter food. But while the young outlaw—for Peleus was only such—sat footsore and hungry on the green turf and watched these wise creatures, how by their industry they waxed rich, there came a sudden flash of lightning and a stunning clap of thunder from the clouds that hovered over Mount Olympus, and, presto! all was changed. The ant-hill was suddenly transformed into a white-walled town, and the insects themselves into busy men and women hurrying through the streets, carrying burdens, building houses, and buying and selling, just as though they had always been used to doing so. Armed warriors stood guard at the gates, and sturdy farmers with their teams of oxen were bringing in the produce of the fields; and in the middle part of the city, surrounded by a garden of olives and pomegranates, was a white palace which the Myrmidons had built for Peleus, whom they now hailed as their king.

But the most interesting happening in the life of King Peleus was his wedding with the sea-nymph Thetis, for that was the starting point of the greatest romance that has ever been sung or written. Whether Thetis was really a silver-footed nymph, as the poets would have us believe, or whether she was only the daughter of a fisherman, it matters not, the time was so long ago. It is certainly true that she was famed all over the world for her beauty and her many graces; and Peleus, who was then too old to be handsome, had no easy time of it in the winning of her.

The wedding was the grandest ever known, for there were gods and heroes among the guests; and the wedding presents, which were brought from land and sea and sky, were such as were never seen before or since. According to the custom of the time, the finest of these gifts were nominally for the bridegroom; but I have little doubt that had it not been for the sake of the beautiful bride they would not have been given. Among these gifts was a suit of well-wrought armor with a wooden tablet attached to it upon which was written: "This is from the gods." There was also an ashen spear of great weight which Cheiron, the Centaur, had cut and shaped from a tree that grew on the topmost crag of Mount Pelion. But the last and best of all were two peerless war steeds called Balios (Swift) and Xanthos (Old-Gold), the gift of the mighty sea-king Poseidon.

Both of these horses were of the same height, both were of the same perfect shape, and they moved together as if they had but one mind. Their color was that of old gold finely burnished, and their long manes, which were like silk for fineness, sparkled like sunbeams in the clear air of a frosty morning. Their eyes were like the eyes of eagles, their feet were light as the air, their speed was that of the west wind, and they understood the language of men.

Perhaps it would be unfair to say that King Peleus was prouder of these horses than he ever expected to be of his fair young wife. He had a fine suite of rooms fitted up for them in his palace at Phthia, and the best grooms in Hellas were employed to take care of them day and night. The fame of the steeds soon spread into foreign lands, and many were the princes and heroes that came from beyond the sea to look at and admire them. But the harness that belonged to them hung unused in its place upon the wall. For old King Peleus, who in his younger days had been a famous rider and driver, and had won the title of Lord of Horses, was too feeble ever to mount the war chariot again, and Swift and Old-Gold were too noble and precious to be driven by any common mortal. Every day they were bathed in wine and washed in the clearest spring water, their manes were oiled and combed and plaited in tresses, and they were allowed to gambol for an hour in the king's orchard. Otherwise they stood idle in their stalls, and knew neither bit nor lash nor loud war-cry; and while their master grew older and feebler with every change of the moon, they remained always young and beautiful and strong.

By and by a son was born to Thetis and the king, a fair-haired child who the soothsayers declared would be greater than his father and yet would die sooner than he. When the babe was brought in the nurse's arms to Peleus, the old man looked upon him fondly and said:

"This is the hero who will drive the steeds Balios and Xanthos in battle. He shall also have the armor of well-wrought bronze which the gods gave me on my wedding day, and the mighty spear which Cheiron, my wise grand-father, hewed out of the mountain-ash."

But the babe, afraid of the gray locks and wrinkled vis-age of its sire, cried; and Peleus, turning away, said: "He is, after all, only a little whiner!" And they therefore called him Ligyron, which means whining.

When Ligyron was yet a very little child, his father sent him to live with Cheiron, who had a famous nursery and kindergarten of heroes at his home on the wooded slopes of Mount Pelion. The wise old Centaur changed the lad's name to Achilles and fed him with the hearts of lions and the marrow of bears and wild boars. And the boy was taught how to use the bow and how to manage horses and how to take care of his own body that he might always be strong and brave. He also learned what were the best ways of treating wounds, and what kind of herbs were good for medicines; and he became inured to exposure and danger, sleeping in the open air, chasing wild boars in the forest, riding barebacked on the half-tamed horses of the plains, and skirmishing with savage robbers in the mountain passes. He was not more than nine years old when, hav-ing finished his course in Cheiron's school, he went back to his home in Phthia, a tall, yellow-haired, sun-browned youth, very quick of temper, strong-limbed, and as grace-ful as he was brave. His fair mother wept when she saw him, for a soothsayer had told her that his life, although a glorious one, should be of short duration. His old father was very proud of him, and took him out to show him the treasures of the palace.

"Here," said the king, "is the matchless armor of bronze which the gods gave me on my wedding day. No man has ever yet worn it, but you are already well-nigh large enough for it to fit you becomingly. See this fair, round shield with many an image of beauty graven upon it, and this helmet with its nodding horsehair plume—was ever anything so delightsome to a young warrior's eye? And here is the ashen spear which not one of our Myrmidons is strong enough to wield, but which your stout arms will soon be able to hurl. And, lastly, here are Swift and Old-Gold, the noblest war steeds that any mortal ever owned. All these things are yours, my son!"

SECOND HEAT—BEFORE TROY

As I have set out to tell you only about a famous team of horses, I shall not be expected to relate the history of that ever-memorable war in which Swift and Old-Gold acted so important a part—the war which the Greeks waged against Troy on the farther side of the Ægean Sea. Hence I shall not stop to explain the causes of that war, how they began at old Peleus's wedding feast and became active when beautiful Helen of Argos was carried away by Prince Paris of Troy. Nor shall I tell how King Agamemnon lighted the war fires on every hilltop of Greece and summoned every warrior chief to join him in defending the honor of their country by punishing the Trojans and bringing fair Helen back to her home. Nor need I relate how the young Achilles was at first hidden away by his mother lest he should go to the war and lose his life therein; nor how, being discovered in his hiding-place, he was afterward persuaded to lead his Myrmidons to the attack upon Troy, although well knowing that he would never return to his native land; nor how nine long years were wasted in desultory warfare along the Trojan shores; nor yet how, at the beginning of the tenth year, Achilles, being angered at Agamemnon's high-handed tyranny, drew off his Myrmidons and withheld his aid at the very time when the Greeks stood most in need of it. Of all these things you may read in the works of the great poets; my story has to do with Swift and Old-Gold and the events that grew out of Achilles's wrath.

A month had already passed since the quarrel, and Achilles sat sulkily in his hut, nursing his anger toward Agamemnon. On either side of him, along the sandy sea-beach, were the tents of his Myrmidons; and behind them, drawn up on the shelving shore just out of reach of the lapping waves, were the fifty black ships which had borne them across the sea. Opening into the same courtyard as their master's hut was the stable wherein Swift and Old-Gold stood lazily champing the clover and parsley which the grooms had cut and brought to them from the meadows along the shore. Three times nine years had passed since they were given to old Peleus at his wedding feast, and yet they were as wondrously fair and strong and swift as they had ever been. Many times since crossing the sea, they had borne their young master into the din and fury of battle, and many times had their fearlessness and his prowess turned the tide of war. But now the days were passed in idleness. Their harness with their master's armor hung useless within the hut. The war chariot, polished and clean, stood well covered up beside the door, and Achilles's mighty ashen spear, leaned, half-forgotten, against the wall. The Myrmidons lolled lazily upon the grass in the shadow of their tents, some sleeping, some playing checkers or games of chance, and some telling wonderful tales of warfare and adventure. But beneath the walls of Troy, only a short distance away, the rest of the Greeks were fighting a losing battle with the Trojans. In vain did Agamemnon and his chiefs urge their warriors to the fray. Their foes, led by brave Hector of Troy, worsted them on every hand, and later in the day drove them back beaten and disheartened to the shore of the sea and to the shelter of their ships.

And the two war steeds, champing clover and gazing out of the open door of the courtyard, talked together about the prospects of the war.

"Methinks," said Swift, "that unless our master takes the field the Greeks will soon be pushed into the sea."

"Agamemnon himself knows that," responded Old-Gold, "and he will send men to Achilles this very night, to persuade him to forget his anger."

"And what will our master do then?" asked Swift. "Tell me, brother, for thou canst sometimes see into the future."

"He will not be moved, for he is unforgiving. And yet he will allow his dear friend Patroclus to lead the Myrmidons into the fight. Have courage, brother, for I smell the fray afar off, and we shall have part in it ere many days."

THIRD HEAT—THE KING'S MESSENGERS

THAT night the men of Troy encamped on the plain between the city and the ships, and Swift and Old-Gold looking out could see a thousand watch-fires blazing, and in the gleam of each sat fifty warriors proudly boasting of their deeds. But the Greeks were cowering among their tents on the shore and debating whether to betake themselves at once to their ships and return in disgrace to their native land, or whether to try the uncertain issue of another day of battle.

"Ah!" cried Swift, peering into the gloom. "Who comes here? It must be the men whom Agamemnon has sent out to treat with our master."

Moving with great caution along the shore, lest they should be heard by some Trojan picket, three noble Greeks were making their way toward the hut of Achilles. They were Ajax, the cousin of Achilles and next to him the mightiest of living heroes; Ulysses, the wiliest of the Grecian chiefs; and knightly old Phoinix, who had once been Achilles's schoolmaster in Phthia. With these men were also two heralds who came to help them find the way. Very quietly did they draw near, led by the cunning Ulysses. Unseen by anyone save the two war steeds, they entered the open door. They crossed the courtyard, found Achilles in his own room playing a sweet air upon a lyre of curious workmanship, and singing of the glories of war, whilst over against him sat his friend Patroclus, silently listening. Surprised by their sudden coming, both of the young men sprang to their feet, Achilles with the lyre still in his hand. Then he welcomed them warmly as his dearest friends, and leading them forward he made them sit down upon soft cushions and carpets of purple, and turning to Patroclus he bade him bring forth a great bowl of mixed wine and a cup for each of his guests.

And Patroclus did this and more. In the light of the blazing fire he placed a great fleshing-block, and upon it he laid a goat's back and choice pieces of mutton and pork; and having sliced them well, he pierced them with spits and roasted them above the hot coals. Then he put the meat on platters, and brought out baskets of white bread which he served to the guests. But Achilles himself served the meat, while Patroclus sacrificed to the gods by throwing some of the choicest pieces into the fire. When all had partaken of the good cheer before them Ulysses filled a cup with wine and pledged it to Achilles and made known the object of their coming.

All night long the three messengers pleaded with Achilles to lay aside his anger and to give to the sorely tried Greeks the succor of which they stood in so great need. And they promised in the name of Agamemnon that he should have for his reward seven tripods untouched by fire, and ten talents of gold, and twenty caldrons of bronze, and twelve prize-winning horses, and seven women slaves skilled in the finest handiwork. More than this, if they should succeed in taking Troy, then Achilles might load his ship full of gold and bronze from the pillage of the palaces; and he might choose the fairest of Agamemnon's daughters for his wife, and take with her as her dower seven well-peopled cities that lay near the sea. But Achilles turned a deaf ear to all their entreaties, and declared that it was his purpose to sail on the morrow with his Myrmidons back to his native land.

"Hateful to me," he said, "are Agamemnon's gifts, and to me he is not worth a straw. Not even if he gave me ten times, yea, twenty times, all that is his and all that may come to him—even though he should promise me gifts in number as the sand, yet he shall not persuade me. And so you have my answer."

And Ajax and Ulysses arose, and went back sorrowfully to their own tents. But old Phoinix stayed with his one-time pupil Achilles.

FOURTH HEAT—THE FIERCE FIGHT

ON the next day, and the next, and the next, the battle raged fiercely about the camp and the ships of the Greeks; but Achilles and his Myrmidons stayed quietly in their tents, and neither gave aid to their countrymen nor embarked on their ships to return to their native land. On the third day, however, Patroclus went out unarmed to see how things were faring with his friends. It was a sad tale that he brought back to Achilles.

"The bravest of the Greeks," said he, "are lying among the ships smitten and wounded. Everywhere the men of Troy press upon them; they have broken over the wall into the camp, and they are even throwing fire into the ships. If thou withhold thy help longer, surely thou art without pity— thou canst not be the son of Peleus and gentle Thetis, but art rather born of the gray sea and the beetling rocks. But if that old prophecy of the soothsayer holds thee back, then I pray thee let me go forth leading the Myrmidons to the help of our kinsmen. And lend me thine armor and chariot and the war steeds, Swift and Old-Gold, so that the Trojans will mistake me for thee and perhaps be dismayed at my coming."

Achilles was moved by his friend's entreaties, and the more so as, looking toward the Grecian ships, he saw thick smoke arise and then great sheets of flame.

"Truly, you may go!" he cried. "Gird on my armor quickly, and I will call the Myrmidons."

Patroclus made haste to don the armor great and fair which the gods had given to old Peleus on his marriage day. Round his shoulders he belted the sword of bronze, on his head he set the glittering helmet, and in his hands he took the mighty shield and two strong lances. But the ashen spear that Cheiron had made he left in the hut, for no man but Achilles could wield it. Then the horses, Swift and Old-Gold, were led out by Automedon, the skillfullest of charioteers, and harnessed in their places. Very glad were the noble steeds when they smelled the battle and knew that they were soon to take part in the dreadful fray. And in the side-traces Automedon put a third horse, a chestnut-colored steed named Pedasos, which had been captured in Cilicia.

In the meanwhile Achilles had called the Myrmidons to arms, and now they came forward in close-serried ranks, shield pressed against shield, helm against helm, and man against man—the horsehair crests on the bright helmet-ridges touching each other when they nodded, so closely together did they stand. And the proud war horses, Swift and Old-Gold, guided by the strong arms of Automedon and drawing the car in which stood the fearless Patroclus, led the way into the thick of battle. And in one mass the Myrmidons fell upon the Trojans that were besetting the ships, and the din of the conflict waxed wondrous great.

Now, when the Trojans saw the chariot drawn by the

world-famous steeds and in it Patroclus shining in armor, they wavered in the fight, for they thought that Achilles himself had come out against them. Then, as if every man sought only his own safety, they turned and in dreadful panic fled as best they could away from the encampment of the Greeks. And wherever they were thickest in the flight, there followed Swift and Old-Gold, glorying in their strength and speed, crushing men beneath their feet, and overturning many a fleeing car. When they came to the great ditch that the Greeks had digged outside their camp, many were the horses and very many the men that fell in one terrible, struggling heap; but our swift steeds, guided by Automedon, leaped straight over all in their mad pursuit of the mighty Hector, who was speeding across the plain toward the shelter of his own gates.

But why tell of all the terrible deeds of that terrible day? Why tell of the fight beneath the walls of Troy, of the brave rallying of the Trojans under great Hector, and of the fierce onset of Sarpedon, who slew the goodly trace-horse Pedasos with his spear? Then indeed it might have gone hard with Patroclus had not Automedon reached over with his long-edged sword and quickly cut adrift the unlucky beast; and Swift and Old-Gold, no longer cumbered in their course, strained forward upon the reins and rushed furiously onward.

At length, however, there was a turn in the tide of battle, for Patroclus, still eager to meet the great Hector, was struck from behind. His helmet was smitten from his head and rolled rattling away beneath the horses' hoofs; the long lance which he bore was shattered in his hands, and the tasseled shield fell with a crash to the ground.

The Greeks afterward said that no mortal dealt that blow, but only Apollo, whom no man can withstand. Dazed and blind and sorely wounded, Patroclus would have fled to the succor of his comrades. But Hector, seeing his sorry plight, now rushed upon him and with his spear gave him his death wound. With a crash the hero fell headlong to the ground, and the swift-footed steeds bore the chariot and Automedon, the driver, away from the field.

Then, throughout the rest of the day, Trojans and Greeks fought around the body of Patroclus, these that they might carry it to the ships, and those that they might drag it in triumph into the city. Swift and Old-Gold, when they had gotten away from the thick of battle and knew their warrior had fallen, would move no farther but stood still and wept. Vainly did Automedon try to coax them with gentle words; vainly did he ply the cruel lash; they would neither go back to the ships nor return to the field of fight. With their heads bowed to the ground, they wept hot tears for Patroclus, and their shining manes were covered with dust. At length, however, as if new courage had been put into their knees, they rallied and made a fierce onset upon the enemy, and behind them Automedon fought wildly, sweeping upon his foes as a vulture upon wild geese. Being alone in the car, however, he could do small harm, for he was unable to wield his spear and at the same time guide his fiery team.

So the fighting went on over the body of Patroclus, from which Hector had already stripped the gory armor, and it was not until the evening that the Greeks were at last able to bear it from the field, and, with the stress of war waxing fierce behind them, carry it in sorrow back to the ships. And Swift and Old-Gold, their heads drooping and their manes bedraggled in dust and blood, returned with Automedon and the battered chariot to the tent of their master Achilles.

FIFTH HEAT—ÆTHON AND GALATHE

THE proudest of all the steeds that went out of the battle that day were Hector's royal horses, Æthon and Galathe. Red as the glowing flame, or as the sunset clouds, was Æthon; yellow as the buttercups that bespangle the meadows, was Galathe; swift as birds on the wing, and tireless as eagles, were they both. They had been reared in the rich pasture-lands of Lycia, some say by Apollo, the archer-god, and had been chosen by their master for their beauty and strength. For ten years they had been fed in the king's own stalls and cared for by the hands of Hector himself, and among all the horses of Troy there were none to be compared with them.

From noon till evening on that eventful day, ever in the thickest of the fight, they had drawn their master's chariot without fear or weariness; and when at length the darkness had put an end to the dreadful combat, it was with high heads and tossing manes that they betook themselves to the camp of the victorious Trojans. They knew that behind them rode the hero of the day, and at his feet lay the armor which he had stripped from Patroclus—the matchless armor which the gods had given to old Peleus. From out of the mêlée of battle they had come unscathed by any wound, and as fresh as when the grooms had led them from their stalls. All through that night they stood beside the chariot in the blazing light of the watch-fires, and champed white barley and spelt, and waited impatiently for the day.

"To-day our master will drive the Greeks into the sea," said red Æthon as the dawn arose behind the distant mountains.

"Yes," said Galathe, "to-day he will rid Troy of her foes. See! he has donned the armor of the gods which he stripped from foolhardy Patroclus. Not even Achilles would dare meet him now."

And when the sun had risen, gilding the towers of Troy with his beams, Hector marshaled his host and mounting his chariot led them forth to battle again.

In the meanwhile the death of Patroclus had wrought a great change in the stubborn heart of Achilles. His wrath toward Agamemnon was laid aside, and he vowed that he would not rest until he had slain Hector and avenged his friend. All night long he sat before the tents and wept, and as soon as morning dawned he hastened to prepare himself for the battle. The armor with which he girded himself was better even than that which he had lost through Patroclus's sad misfortune. For it had been wrought by Vulcan, the lame blacksmith of the gods, and its likeness for beauty and service had never been seen. When he had proved the armor to see whether it fitted him, he took in hand the ashen spear, great and heavy and strong, which Cheiron had given to his father and which none of the Greeks could wield. Forthwith the grooms led out his war steeds. They buckled on the breast-straps and put bits into their mouths and stretched the reins behind to the chariot. Then Automedon sprang up into his place, ready to drive to the field of combat, and Achilles, armed in his sun-bright coat of mail, stepped into the car.

"Xanthos and Balios, Swift and Old-Gold," he cried, "take heed that you bring your charioteer safe back to his tent and to his own folk, and do not leave him on the field as you left Patroclus!"

Then Old-Gold bowed his head to the ground until his long mane fell over his eyes and face, and said: "Truly, great master, we will bear thee safe this day, but yet thy death is not far away. It was through no fault of ours that the Trojans slew good Patroclus, but by the will of the gods. And so, too, shall thy own fate overtake thee."

Achilles was sorely troubled by these words, for never before had he heard aught of speech from the lips of the horse. "Xanthos," he cried, "why do you tell me of my death? I know that I shall never return to my old father and beautiful mother and dear native land; and therefore I will not hold my hand until I have avenged my friend." And having spoken, he rode onward, leading his Myrmidons and the hosts of the Greeks into the battle.

I need not follow the events of this day, a day in which the tide of war was turned and the Trojans forced to flee into the city for their lives. It was with downcast heads that Æthon and Galathe dragged their master's chariot within the gates that afternoon, and their eyes no longer flashed with joy and pride. The terror of Achilles had cowed them utterly, as it had the entire Trojan host, and they knew that they had borne their master into the fight for the last time.

On the high battlements of Troy a sorrowful company was gathered—the king, the queen, and such of the Trojan princes as the fortunes of war had spared—and they wept and wailed and tore their garments for grief at the sad sight which they beheld outside of the walls. For Hector, the flower and hope of Troy, had been slain at the hands of Achilles. Despoiled of his armor, he lay bound to the tail of the victor's chariot, his head trailing in the dust. The pitiless lord of the Myrmidons stood in the car alone, and lashed his steeds to their utmost speed, and Swift and Old-Gold, unused to such cruelty, leaped wildly in their traces and flew over the plain with the swiftness of the wind, while a cloud of dust arose about them as if to hide their master's heartless deed from the eyes of the pitying beholders.

Hector's mother shrieked aloud in her grief, and tore her long hair, and threw her veil far over the wall. The king, his father, moaned piteously, and would have gone out alone from the gates to entreat the mercy of Achilles, had not those around him held him back. And the cries of the people upon the walls were echoed throughout the town, and there was mourning and wild grief in every house. Around the entire circuit of the city, Achilles drove his team, and then, followed by his Myrmidons and with the body of Hector still trailing in the dust, he betook himself to his own encampment beside the sea.

Then Hector's squire, heavy of heart because of that day's work, went out into his master's courtyard and un-yoked the steeds Æthon and Galathe, and led them away from the blood-stained chariot which they had drawn so often to victory.

"Never again," said he, "shall you bear your master into the field of strife; never again shall you lift your proud heads in joy. Better would it have been had we all been slain, for there is no longer any hope for Troy."

Then he washed them in clear water, and combed their

A GREEK WAR CHARIOT.

manes as he had been used to do, and fed them with parsley and white barley. But they never drew war car again.

SIXTH HEAT—THE THREAD OF FATE

THAT night, as Swift and Old-Gold stood in their stalls, champing sweet clover and looking out into the darkness, they saw a strange procession coming slowly across the meadows and drawing near to the spacious hut which the Myrmidons had built for their master Achilles. The sentinels had fallen asleep at their posts, and the warriors, weary and worn, had retired within their tents. The great chief himself, having closed and bolted the heavy outer door of his hut, was sitting at meat with his squire Automedon.

"Who is it that rides unchallenged toward our door?" asked Swift.

"Methinks," answered Old-Gold, "that it is old King Priam of Troy, coming in his sorrow to beg the body of his son Hector, which lies uncared for in our courtyard. I see in front a smooth-running wagon drawn by the two strong mules which the Mysians gave to the king in his happier days. All the world knows those mules, for they have never been matched in strength and endurance. On the wagon I see chests of gold and much fine bronze, which I suppose the old man is bringing to offer as a ransom for his dead son. And yoked to the king's light car that follows behind are two sad steeds with drooping ears and lifeless gait. If I am not mistaken, the dull-coated creatures are Æthon and Galathe, the once proud creatures that drew Prince Hector into the battle."

Soon the wagon and the chariot drew up before the door, and the king and his groom dismounted. With them was also a herald, whose armor shone brightly amid the gloom, and whom neither Swift nor Old-Gold had ever seen before. The great door was barred with a huge bolt made of a log of pine, so heavy that three stout Greeks could barely move it, although Achilles alone could thrust it home. But the bright herald easily pushed it aside and opened the door without making any noise; and then, having bidden the king good-by, he as silently disappeared in the darkness.

"I do believe that he is Hermes, the kind messenger of the gods," said Old-Gold.

King Priam left the groom to mind the horses and the mules, and went boldly across the courtyard into the room where his great enemy sat; nor was Achilles aware of his coming till he saw him standing silently before him. As the warrior leaped astonished to his feet, the old king clasped his knees and entreated his pity, and reminded him of his own dear father Peleus in his lonely palace in far-off Phthia. And the heart of Achilles was strangely stirred within him as he remembered his boyhood and his native land and his sorrowing parents, to whom he should never return; and he gave kind heed to Priam's petition, and the two lifted up their voices together and wept.

"This," said Achilles, "is the thread of fate which the gods have spun for miserable men, that they should live in sorrow. For although they gave to Peleus splendid gifts, and favored him above all other men, yet they meted out to him great grief because no princely sons were born in his halls save only myself, who am doomed to an untimely death."

Then Priam besought him that, for the sake of his own father (so soon to be bereaved), he would deliver to him the body of Hector and accept therefor the rich ransom that he had brought. Without saying a word in reply, Achilles, followed by his squire, hastened across the courtyard and leaped through the great door. Then, loosing the horses and the mules, they began to unload the countless treasures. And when they had carried all into the house, they took up the body of Hector from the place where it lay, and, having covered it over with a doublet and a princely robe and laid it upon a bier, they lifted it into the polished wagon.

Long before the dawn of day, Swift and Old-Gold, still looking out into the darkness, saw the chariot of King Priam and the wagon drawn by the team of mules issue noiselessly from the courtyard. And in the chariot stood the king and his groom; but upon the wagon, driving the sturdy mules, sat the bright herald whom Old-Gold declared to be none other than Hermes, the helper of men, come down to aid the old man in his dire extremity. And upon the bier behind, covered with heavy robes, was all that remained of the mighty Hector.

"They go thus early for fear of the Greeks, who are crafty above all other men," said Old-Gold. Then the steeds returned to their manger of sweet clover.

And at sunrise, at a little distance outside of the city gates, all the people of Troy met Priam bringing home his dead.

SEVENTH HEAT—THE GOAL

BUT the doom of Achilles, which the soothsayer had foretold at his birth, came sure and soon. One day, while hard fighting was going on beneath the walls of Troy, he drove his chariot close up to the famous gate, called the Scæan, and stopped to taunt the unhappy Trojans who stood upon the battlements. Vainly did the faithful steed, Old-Gold, champ upon his foaming bit and rear in his traces and strain hard upon the reins; for he knew the fate that threatened his master and would fain have carried him away from danger. But Achilles, standing high in the chariot, boasted of his great deeds: how from the sea he had laid waste twelve cities, and from the land eleven; how he had vanquished the queen of the Amazons, and had slain Hector, the hope of the Trojans; how he had taken great spoils and countless treasures from many lands; and how, in all the world, there was no name so terrible as his, no, not even the name of the sun-bright Apollo.

But scarcely had the last rash boast passed his lips when a gleaming spear circled down upon him from above, nor could the armor which Vulcan had forged for him ward off the swift death which it brought. Some say that the fatal weapon was hurled from the battlements by Paris, the perfidious prince who had caused all that sad war; and others assert that it came from the hands of no mortal man, but was cast from the sky by great Apollo himself, offended beyond measure at the hero's boasting. I do not know whether either of these stories is true, nor does it matter now. All I need to say is that the destroyer of three and twenty cities fell headlong and helpless in the dust, as many another boaster has done since his day, and the great world went on as before. And his wonderful war steeds, no longer restrained by his voice and hand, sprang wildly away and galloped with the speed of the wind across the plain.

And old King Peleus, rich and wretched, the favorite of the gods, sat mourning in his desolate halls at Phthia. But his hero son never returned to him, and no man brought him any word concerning the fate of the rare gifts which Poseidon had given him on his wedding day—the immortal creatures, Swift and Old-Gold.

THE GREAT WOODEN HORSE

I. THE PUZZLED TROJANS

OF all the wooden horses that men have ever made, he was the hugest. Yet he was not very handsome. Built hastily of rough-hewn maple planks and of beams and spars from the wrecks of unseaworthy ships, the great wonder is that he was so well made. But old Epeus, who planned and directed the building of the huge fellow, was a master-carpenter, the skillfullest in the world; and the rough pieces of timber were fitted together with such nicety that there was no crack, nor crevice, nor point of weakness, in any part of the work. Certain men who were jealous of Epeus's fame whispered that it was not he, but the goddess Athena, who did it all; and this we shall not deny.

Early one morning the people of Troy were astonished to learn that the Greeks, who had been besieging their city for ten weary years, had sailed away during the night. Nobody had seen them go, nobody knew whither they had gone; but anybody, by climbing up to the watchtower above the Scæan gate, could see that they had utterly vanished. The sandy beach where a thousand ships had been drawn up was deserted and bare, save that it was strewn with the ruins of the huts and tents that had so long sheltered the persistent Greeks. A short distance to the left, and half concealed behind a growth of tall reeds, was a dark object

which puzzled the Trojan watchmen not a little. When first
seen in the gray light of the dawn, it looked like some huge
sea-monster, black and slimy, just emerged from the water.

"Great Neptune is with us!" cried one of the men. "He
has sent a creature out of the deep, and it has swallowed
up our enemies and their tents and their ships, and left
not one to tell the tale."

"Nonsense!" said another, who had sharper eyes. "This
thing looks to me like no creature at all, but rather a statue
of some kind which the Greeks have built, and left behind
them as a token of their disappointment and defeat. And
now I remember that I have seen crowds of them busy at
work on the same spot for several days. I have no doubt
but that they are all far over the sea by this time, and this
east wind will waft them swiftly to their own country."

All Troy, when it awoke and heard the glad news,
stretched itself out and took a long breath. The shopkeep-
ers threw open their doors and hung up their handsomest
goods where they would catch the eyes of the passers-by.
The farmers brought out their plows and mended their
old harness and talked about the big crops they would
raise in the fields that had lain fallow so long and had been
enriched with so much human blood. The housewives
returned to their long-neglected spinning, or overhauled
their linen closets, and brushed the cobwebs out of their
bed-chambers. The citizen-soldiers hung up their bows and
quivers, their swords and shields, and each began to furbish
up the instruments of his trade. The maidens donned their
best gowns and went out to walk and smile sweetly. The
small boys with their fishing-lines in their pockets, and the
great crowd of idlers who always expected to grow rich

upon what they could find, hastened into the streets and elbowed their way to the gates, only to find them closed.

About noon, however, the gate next to the sea was thrown wide open. A great multitude poured out, and the mad race that was made for the shore was like the scramble of boomers on our Western frontier when lands are given away by the Government. Soon thousands were on the beach, looking eagerly for whatever the Greeks might have dropped, but seldom finding anything more valuable than a broken comb, a bit of leather, or some small pieces of crockery. All were shy of the southern part of the beach, where the strange monster stood among the reeds. Everybody could plainly see now that it was a horse. Its huge head, its arching neck, its broad back, its flowing tail, were visible from every part of the beach; and the boys who had ventured nearest said that it stood firmly on a broad platform of planks.

That it was an immense horse, and that it was made of wood, nobody could dispute. But why had the Greeks built it, and why had they left it there? Presently a number of the king's counselors came out to look at the strange object and decide what to do with it. Some advised that it should be drawn into the city and lodged within the tower, there to be a kind of permanent exposition of the folly of the Greeks. Others were in favor of throwing it into the sea, or of kindling a fire beneath it and burning it to ashes.

The dispute would doubtless have ended in blows had not Laocoön, a prince of Troy and priest of Apollo, come hastily out from the city with a small company of soldiers.

"What folly is this?" he cried. "Who wants to take anything into the city that the Greeks have left upon our shores?

As for my part, I would look with dread upon any gift that they might offer us. This horse is not so harmless as he looks. Either there are armed men within his giant body, or he is so put together that when he is taken into the city he will fly into pieces, knock down our walls, and destroy our houses. Throw him into the sea, burn him to ashes, do anything but receive him within our walls."

Having said this, he hurled his heavy spear at the monster. The weapon struck it full in the breast, where it remained quivering, and those who stood nearest fancied that they heard deep hollow groans issuing from the throat of the beast.

"To the sea with him! To the sea with him!" cried a hundred voices.

"What a fine blaze he will make!" cried others. And they ran hither and thither gathering sticks and driftwood with which to kindle a fire beneath him.

II. THE CAPTURED GREEK

IN great danger then was the sturdy beast, and the Trojans would have made an end of him right quickly had not something happened to change their minds. Suddenly a great hubbub was heard some distance down the beach, and men and boys, forgetting the horse for the moment, ran hurriedly to the spot to see what was going on. A party of peasants were dragging toward the city a young man who, covered with mud and blood, and with his hands tied behind him, seemed a target for every kind of insult. His clothing told that he was a Greek.

"Hold on!" cried one of the king's counselors. "Bring the fellow here, and stop your noise. We will see what he can tell us about his friends and this strange monster that they have left on our shores. Who are you, wretch, and where are your people who so lately were encamped on this very spot?"

"My name," said the captive, "is Sinon, and I am by birth a Greek. But people I have none; for the Greeks have condemned me to death, and now ye Trojans also seek my life. Where, indeed, shall I turn when kinsmen and foes would alike slay me?"

These words, spoken in sweet and persuasive tones, touched the hearts of the rude rabble, and they paused to hear what further the young man would say.

"Speak on," said the king's counselor, "and tell us by what cruel fate you have been left behind by your countrymen to fall into the hands of your foes."

"It is a long story," responded the young man, "but I will not weary you. For more than a year the crafty Ulysses has been plotting my destruction, and for no other reason than because I once befriended a chief whom he dislikes. When, at length, three months ago, the Greeks decided in council to give up this war and return to their own land, he saw his opportunity. Storms swept across the sea, and the south wind brought tempests in its train, and the ships dared not leave their moorings. Then the chiefs called together the soothsayers and asked them what should be done to appease the gods, that so they might have favorable winds and a smooth sea for their homereturning voyage. And one of them, Eurypylus, declared that nothing short of a human sacrifice would turn aside the vengeful ire of Apollo; the other, Calchas, explained that since the Greeks had stolen the statue of Athena which stood in your great temple of Troy, that goddess would never suffer them to return to their native land until they had reared on these shores the massive figure of a horse to be a witness to their repentance. Then the chiefs asked who should be the victim to be offered up to Apollo. And Calchas, urged on by Ulysses, answered 'Sinon.' Forthwith, I was bound with cords, fillets were tied about my temples, and the knife was sharpened ready to pierce my heart. But on the night before the rueful day, I burst my bonds and escaped to the slimy marshes, where I lay hidden until I saw my countrymen embark and sail away in their thousand ships across the sea to distant Greece. Then, almost dead from hunger and privation, I ventured out, only to be seized by these rude peasants and dragged to this place as you see me now."

"But the horse—the horse!" cried the Trojans. "What about the horse?"

"I have already told you," answered Sinon, "that the image was built to appease the wrath of the goddess Athena. The soothsayers declared that not only would it bless its builders, but that into whatever city it should go, there it would carry good fortune and peace and prosperity. The Greeks, however, were unwilling that it should bring happiness to you, their foes, and hence they built it very large, and so tall that it cannot pass through any of your gates; and they placed it here close to the reedy marsh, in the hope that, when the autumn rains fell and the sea raged furiously, the waves would beat upon and overwhelm it and carry it away, and no people whatever should be blessed by its presence."

"Ah! That is their game, is it?" cried the Trojans with

one voice. "Well, we'll see about that. We'll have the good horse inside our walls this very night."

Then there was great shouting and rejoicing on every side, and those who had been the first to wreak their spite upon Sinon were the first to undo his bonds and wipe the blood from his face, and find food for him to eat. Forthwith two companies of men were sent to the city, one to bring long, strong ropes, and the other to make a breach in the wall large enough to allow the great horse to be drawn through.

III. THE FATE OF LAOCOÖN

IN the meanwhile a fearful tragedy was being enacted on the beach. Laocoön, the priest of Apollo, had built an altar on the sands and was making ready to offer up a sacrifice, as had been the custom of his country from ancient times. His two sons stood beside him, one on either hand, ready to do their part. Suddenly loud shouts arose from those who were nearest the sea, and everybody fled in dismay. Looking out toward the island of Tenedos, Laocoön saw two huge serpents swimming with wondrous speed toward the land. He smiled at the cowardly fears of the people, and would not desert the altar which he had raised. He doubtless thought that the reptiles were mere water-snakes, and that they would not venture upon the land. But in this he was sadly mistaken, for upon reaching the beach the serpents reared their heads high in the air and glided with the swiftness of light over the sands. Ere Laocoön and his boys could make a single movement toward escape, the horrid creatures had reached the altar; they had twined their slimy folds around the necks and limbs of the three unfortunates; they had crushed them to death in their terrible embrace. The people who saw this awful tragedy from a distance were spellbound with horror, nor did they know who might be the next victim. But the serpents, when they had done their deadly work, glided quietly away and hid themselves beneath an altar which the Greeks had erected to Athena.

"Behold the vengeance of the goddess!" cried some of the people.

"She has punished Laocoön for his wickedness in smiting the great horse with his spear!" cried others.

"Such be the fate of all who would try to thwart the will of the ever-living powers!" cried the priests. "Let us hasten to appease Athena by drawing her horse into the city and giving it the shelter which it ought to have."

IV. THE SUCCESS OF THE STRATAGEMS

BY this time the men who had been sent after ropes had returned, bringing also stout wheels to be placed underneath the platform whereon the horse stood. With infinite trouble a slip-knot was thrown over the huge wooden head, and long ropes were attached to each of the fore legs. Then, with the aid of levers and pulleys, the whole huge mass was lifted a little at a time, and the smooth-sliding wheels were fastened in their places, one under each corner of the platform. This being done, as many as could get near enough seized hold of the ropes, the word of command was given, and the three long lines of tugging men and boys moved slowly over the plain, dragging the horse behind them. When they drew near the city the whole populace came out to meet them, and the glad shouts which rent the air seemed louder than the cries which warriors utter on the field of battle.

A wide breach had been opened in the wall, and through this, just as the sun was dipping into the sea, the horse was pushed into the city. Once, when the huge body struck against a projecting stone, the Trojans who were nearest were astonished to hear a sound like the rattling of shields, and some turned pale, and looked around with dread, and forgot to join in the chorus of song that was raised in welcome to the image that was to bring peace and good fortune to Troy. Soon darkness came, and the tired people hastened to their homes. Not a soldier remained to guard the broken wall, not a watchman stayed at his post above the gates. Worn out with the excitement of the day, everybody retired early to rest.

About midnight a man crept stealthily along the dark streets, and came finally to the breach that had been made in the wall. With a little lantern and a kettle of pitch in one hand, he climbed up the rough stones to the top. Once there, he sat down for a moment and gazed steadily toward the sea. The moon, now just rising behind him, lighted up the great expanse of water, and he could plainly see not only the long line of beach with the waves rippling upon the sand, but the dark outline of Tenedos Island lying in the shadows four miles farther away. But what did he see between the island and the shore? A thousand ships with their dark hulls just visible above the water, and all propelled by twenty thousand oars that glinted strangely in the moonlight as they rose and fell. The Greeks, who had lain hidden all day behind Tenedos, were returning to the Trojan shore—in a few minutes their vessels would be drawn up in their old places along the white beach.

The man on the wall seemed greatly pleased with what he saw. Rising again to his feet, he hung the kettle of pitch by a chain upon the outside of the wall and into it he dropped a bit of blazing pine which he had lighted with his lantern. Soon a lurid flame arose from the burning mass. It lighted up the plain and was reflected upon the top of the wall, showing the face of the man. It was Sinon, the young Greek.

Immediately answering lights appeared on the ships, and Sinon clambered hastily to the ground. The huge figure of the wooden horse loomed up in the moonlight before him. With the flat of his sword he struck each of its legs three times. Then suddenly there was a great sound of rattling armor above him. The creature seemed to be strangely endowed with life. In a moment there was a noise as of the shooting of bolts and the grating of hinges; a narrow door was opened in the horse's breast, and a gleaming helmet, with a man's face beneath it, was thrust out.

"Is that you, Sinon?"

"It is I, Ulysses."

"Is all well?"

"All is well. The ships are already drawn up upon the sands. The Greeks are marching across the plain. The witless Trojans are asleep and dream not of danger."

Then a rope was let down from the open door, and Ulysses, fully armed, slid hand over hand to the ground. Other heroes followed, all incased in armor, and all right glad to escape from their prison house.

"The trick has succeeded even better than any of us hoped," said Ulysses. "And now for the last act in this long and weary war! Let fire and sword do their work!"

I need not tell how the gates were thrown open to the Greeks, nor how the Trojans were awakened from their dreams of peace only to meet death at the hands of their foes, nor how the torches were applied to palace and hut and the whole city was wrapped in flames. The horse had nothing to do with all this. Amid the smoke and fire, and the din of rattling arms and the shouts of the victors, he stood all the rest of the night and through the morning hours. Toward noon, however, Ulysses and Sinon, passing by the spot, observed that he had disappeared. Whether, in the confusion, Athena had claimed him and carried him away, or whether he had been mysteriously endowed with life and had galloped out of the burning city to find refuge in the woods and mountains, neither of these heroes could tell.

THE HORSE OF BRASS

CAMBUSCAN was the noblest ruler in all the East. On the day upon which he completed the twentieth year of his reign, he held a great feast in his palace, to which all the princes of his realm were invited. The royal dining-hall was a marvel of beauty and magnificence, and the table was the finest that the world has ever seen. At the head of the board sat the king, with his wife Elfeta, his two sons, Algarsif and Camballo, and his daughter Canace. On either side were ranged, in the order of their rank, the noblest lords and the most beautiful ladies of the land. The minstrels played sweet music, and the hearts of the king and his guests were filled with joy.

In the midst of the festivity there came into the hall, without invitation or announcement, a strange knight mounted upon a steed of brass, and holding in his hand a broad, bright mirror. By his side hung a jewel-hilted sword, and on his thumb was a ring of dazzling beauty. Everybody was so astonished that the hall became suddenly silent; the laughter ceased, the minstrels forgot their music, and the guests turned about in their places to gaze at the unexpected sight. The horse walked straight toward the dais where the king sat, and when he was within speaking distance paused. Then the knight saluted the king and queen and lords with a grace and courtesy which none of them had ever seen excelled, and with a manly voice delivered his message.

"The king of Araby and of Ind, whose servant I am," said he, "sends salutations to you. He has also sent to you, O king, in honor of your anniversary, this horse of brass, which can in the space of four and twenty hours bear you without danger into whatsoever part of the world you may wish to go. Or if you choose to soar aloft as an eagle, and look down from the mountain-tops, he will carry you thither. The whole thing is as simple as turning a pin. This sword is also a present to you from my king. It has an edge so keen and sharp that it will cut through the heaviest armor, and no metal can withstand its stroke. And yet it has another property that makes it even more valuable; for, should any man be wounded with it, you can immediately heal him by passing the flat part of it over the wound. This mirror and the ring are for your daughter, fair Canace. In the mirror she can see everything that is going on in your kingdom, and can even read the thoughts of her lover. And while wearing the ring she will understand the language of all the birds, and be able to answer them in their own manner of speaking."

Then the knight, having delivered his message, turned his steed around and rode out into the courtyard. Having dismounted, he was conducted, by the king's command, back into the banquet-hall, where a place was made for him at the feast. But the horse of brass stood in its place immovable, the center of a gaping, wondering crowd. It was as tall and well-proportioned as the famous steeds of Lombardy, and as handsome and light of limb as the finest horses of Polish breed. Some said that it was such a steed as the fairies ride; others that it was Pegasus, the winged steed of Grecian story; still others declared that it looked like the great horse which Epeus contrived for the destruction of the Trojan people; and they feared that armed men might somehow be hidden within it. But the greater number were agreed that it was the skilful work of the Arabic magicians, and hence would better not be tampered with by ignorant hands.

Cambuscan, when he had done feasting, went out into the courtyard, with all his lords and ladies, to look at the wonderful gift which the king of Araby had sent him.

"I pray you," said he to the knight who had brought it, "tell us how to manage this strange creature."

"There is but little to tell," said the knight, laying his hand upon the horse, which began to skip and prance in the strangest manner possible. "When you wish to ride anywhere you have simply to remove this peg which you see between his ears, mount him, and name the place. He will carry you thither by the shortest route, and without ever missing his way. When you wish him to stop, or to descend to the ground, turn this wooden pin half way round, and he will do your bidding. Or, if you wish him to leave you for a time, turn this iron pin, and he will vanish out of sight, and come to you again when he is called by name. Ride when and where you please, he will always be ready to obey."

The king was wonderfully pleased, and resolved that on the morrow he would ride out to see the world. Then he ordered the groom of the bedchamber to take off the horse's jeweled bridle and carry it into the strong room of the palace, where it should be locked up among his costliest treasures. This being done, he gave a sudden turn to the iron pin, as he had been directed, and the horse vanished from sight. The knight, too, had disappeared from the palace, and King Cambuscan remembered when it was too late that he had not told him how or by what name to call the magic steed.

If any one will go to Sarra in Tartary—wherever that may be—and shout the right name of the horse of brass, I doubt not but that he is still waiting to appear. And what more wonderful piece of mechanism could any one wish to own?

THE ENCHANTED HORSE OF FIROUZ SCHAH

ON the first day of the year, which is called Nevrouz, the king of Persia held a great feast in his palace, to which, according to the custom of the country, he invited every man in the world who had perfected any useful or curious invention. As a matter of course, his halls were crowded with ingenious gentlemen from every country of Asia, each more anxious to exhibit the product of his mind and hand than to partake of the delicate viands with which his tables were loaded. Here were men with improved mouse-traps; men with new kinds of sandals; men who were on the point of discovering perpetual motion; alchemists with bottles of the precious elixir of life; authors, threadbare and penniless, who thought they had written something new; schoolmasters with machines for pouring learning into the brains of their pupils; and crowds of enchanters and charlatans, every one of whom had discovered something wherewith he would finally upset the universe. The king was greatly delighted at his success in bringing together so many inventors and so complete a collection of inventions, and he examined with the greatest care the various machines that were submitted to his inspection. The thing which attracted his attention most was an artificial horse made by an ingenious Hindoo—the like of which had never before been seen in Persia.

"Is he alive?" asked the king, struck by the wonderfully natural appearance of the machine.

"He is more alive than either you or I," answered the Hindoo; "for, while we are constantly dying, and would die outright were we not sustained by the food which we eat, he is always strong and hearty, and needs no food. And he is always ready for service. At my command he will carry me across the broadest seas or over the highest mountains, and that without any fatigue.

"That seems to be impossible," said the king.

"I am ready to prove it to you," was the answer.

"You shall do so. Do you see yonder white mountain, whose top seems to pierce the clouds, and which glistens so brightly in the sunlight? On the farther slope of that mountain there grows a palm-tree, the leaves of which are different from any others in the world. Suppose you mount your horse, and, if he can do what you claim, bring me within an hour one of those palm leaves."

"It shall be as you desire," cried the Hindoo, leaping into the saddle. The horse rose swiftly into the air, and then soared away in the direction of the distant mountain.

In less than a quarter of an hour the Hindoo stood before the king, with the palm leaf in his hand.

"Have I not proved the truth of my words concerning the horse?" he asked.

"Most certainly you have," answered the king; "and I rather think that I should like to own such a horse myself."

"It would, indeed, be very convenient for you," answered the Hindoo. "For whenever you wished to see what was going on in the remotest corner of your kingdom, you would have nothing to do but mount your steed, and he would carry you whithersoever you bade him."

"What is the price of the creature?"

"The price? Ah, your majesty, he is so incomparable a steed that I dare not name the price—it must necessarily be so great."

"But it is not so great that the King of Persia cannot pay it if he choose to do so. Out with it, I command you."

"Will your majesty pardon me beforehand for whatever presumption I may appear to have in naming the price?"

"I pardon you, even if you should ask the half of my kingdom. But remember that I do not promise to pay you what you may name."

"The price, then, O king, is the hand of your daughter, fair Nourmahal," said the Hindoo. "Give her to me as my wife, and you shall have this incomparable horse which will make you the most famous monarch in all Asia."

The king did not know what to say. He was angry at the very thought of having a Hindoo for his son-in-law; and yet he had set his mind on the horse, and he feared that if he refused to buy it some other prince might become its possessor. While he was pondering over the matter and disputing with the Hindoo, his son, Firouz Schah, came in.

"I am ashamed of you, father," cried the prince, "that you should hesitate a moment as to what answer this fellow should have. Only think of his impudence in asking to become a member of our family!" With these words the hot-headed youth gave the Hindoo a blow that sent him reeling against the wall. Then, mounting the horse, the prince twisted the peg which was half concealed in its mane, and the creature carried him swiftly up into the air and was soon sailing away to the southward.

The unfortunate Hindoo was filled with alarm for the safety, no less of the horse than of the foolish Firouz Schah.

He threw himself at the feet of the king and prayed that no blame should be imputed to him for any accident that might befall the prince.

"He knows nothing about the machine, not even how to bring it to the earth again," he cried. "If he should lose his life through his own rashness, I beg that I may not be held accountable."

It was some time before the king could fully realize what had happened, for he was naturally rather slow of comprehension. When, however, he was made to understand that there was no way of overtaking the horse or of aiding the prince, he was beside himself with grief and rage. He commanded his attendants to seize the trembling Hindoo and to cast him into prison; and he declared that if his son, Firouz Schah, did not return within twenty days the head of the culprit should be forfeited.

I need not relate how Firouz Schah fared in that first perilous flight of his, nor need I stop to tell of his adventures in India and far-off Bengal, to which the enchanted steed carried him. On the nineteenth day, as his father the king was sitting pensive and sad in his palace, the prince suddenly appeared before him. The king was alarmed at first, thinking that it was a ghost; but when Firouz Schah spoke to him, and assured him that he was alive and well, he greeted him with the greatest show of affection, and begged him to relate the story of his adventures. The young man gave a most romantic account of what had happened to him, and concluded by saying that he had brought with him from the south the most beautiful lady in all the world, the fair princess of Bengal. She had ridden behind him on the enchanted steed and was now at the king's country house, two leagues from the city, waiting until Firouz Schah could obtain permission to lead her home as his bride.

The king was delighted at this prospect of an alliance with the powerful sultan of Bengal, and having again embraced his son he made proclamation that the wedding should occur at once; and preparations were begun for bringing the princess to the palace and giving her a magnificent welcome. As the Hindoo had been the unwitting means of bringing all this happiness and good fortune to Firouz Schah and his father, it was decided that he should be allowed to leave the prison, and, taking the enchanted horse, which was his own property, to depart unharmed from Persia.

"But be sure that you never set foot in our territories again," said the prince; "for I have not yet forgiven you for your impudent proposal to become my brother-in-law."

The Hindoo was glad enough to get his freedom and his horse, but he was angered beyond measure at the insults which the prince had heaped upon him, and he meditated revenge. He mounted the enchanted steed, which seemed to be none the worse for his adventure with Firouz Schah, and flew away. But he had observed the preparations that were being made for the wedding, and he had learned that the princess of Bengal was at the king's country house, waiting for the coming of the prince at the head of a royal procession to conduct her to the palace in the city. He would have his revenge. He accordingly alighted at the king's country house, where he announced himself as a messenger who had been sent by Firouz Schah to carry the princess into the city. He had no difficulty in persuading the young lady to mount behind on the steed which had already borne her safely from the distant country of Bengal. Then they rose high in the air and hovered for a while above the very road along which the prince and his retinue were passing. Imagine, if you can, the rage and despair of Firouz Schah as, glancing upward, he saw his betrothed carried away, he knew not whither, by the revengeful Hindoo. But he was well aware that neither rage nor despair would rescue her from the villain. He therefore returned with all speed into the city, and, having disguised himself as a dervish, set off on a long and well-nigh hopeless pilgrimage in search of some trace of the lost princess.

For weeks and months the faithful Firouz Schah wandered hither and thither, but he heard not a word of the enchanted horse and his riders. He visited every city of Persia; he wandered through the deserts of Bokhara; he traveled eastward into the mountainland of Tibet—eagerly inquiring for news, but everywhere meeting with disappointment. Coming at last into the capital of Kashmir, he heard something which gave him a ray of hope.

"A princess of Bengal, is it?" said a beggar to whom he had given alms, and of whom he had asked the usual question. "No, I have never seen one—nor even an enchanted horse. But our sultan was on the point of marrying a princess of Bengal not long ago. She was wonderfully beautiful, they said. The wedding feast was all ready, and the guests were in the palace, when the princess was suddenly stricken with madness. She was as fierce as any Bengal tiger. It was worth a man's life to go near her. All that could be done, was to shut her up in her room; and there she remains to this day, staring mad, although as beautiful as ever. The sultan has offered a great reward to any physician who will cure her of her malady, but she is so wild that there isn't a physician in Kashmir who dares enter her room."

Firouz did not wait to hear anything more. He hurried away to his lodgings, and having exchanged his dervish costume for the dress of a physician, he presented himself at the sultan's palace. Passing through the courtyard, his heart gave a great leap of joy, for he saw that which made him feel sure he had reached the end of his quest. In a pile of lumber and cast-away furniture he recognized the enchanted horse. To the sultan, who demanded his business, he explained that he was a Persian physician who had given all the years of his life to the study of insanity in its various forms; and he said that, having heard of the madness of the princess of Bengal, he had come to Kashmir in the hope that he might be able to restore her to her senses. The sultan was overjoyed, and yet he warned the pretended physician that no one could enter into the princess's apartment except at the risk of bruised face, broken bones, and even life itself. But Firouz was in no wise daunted by this information.

"I am somewhat of a wizard," said he, "and if I can only allow the princess to catch a glimpse of me before she flies into a fury, I think I can manage the rest."

And so it was done. The door of the princess's apartment was opened very gently. The physician turned his face squarely toward her and pronounced the magic words "Firouz Schah." The maniac became at once as gentle as a lamb, and, instead of tearing out the physician's eyes, greeted him with a most wonderful cordiality. The attendants ran to the sultan declaring that a miracle had been performed, and during their absence the princess hurriedly explained to her lover all that had befallen her since the perfidious Hindoo had carried her away on the enchanted horse. She and her captor had alighted, she said, at a little distance from the city of Kashmir for the purpose of procuring food before continuing their flight into India. There they were discovered by a company of soldiers, who killed the Hindoo and carried her, together with the enchanted horse, into the city. The sultan had no sooner set his eyes upon her than he resolved to make her his wife. Apartments were given to her in the palace, a great wedding-feast was made ready, and—

"I know the rest!" cried Firouz Schah. "And now for the escape!"

A moment later the attendants returned, and with them the sultan, trembling alternately with fear and hope—fear that the princess might scratch his eyes out; hope that the physician had restored her to her senses. And well might he fear, for no sooner did the princess see him than all her fierceness returned, and had not the physician closed the door very quickly there is no knowing what might have happened.

"I find," said he to the sultan, "that the lady's madness was caused by having touched something that was enchanted, perhaps at or about the time that she was brought into Kashmir. If that object can be found, and she can be induced to touch it again, there is no doubt but that she will recover at once. Otherwise, the case appears to me to be a hopeless one."

"Touched something enchanted!" said the sultan. "What could it have been? I cannot think of anything."

Then he called the officers of his household together

and made inquiry of them: "Do you know of any enchanted object that could have been in the way of the princess of Bengal on the evening that she was brought into Kashmir?"

None of them knew of any such thing. But by and by one, who had been with the soldiers when they killed the Hindoo, remembered that there was an old horse brought into town—a curious old wooden horse, covered with a horse's hide, which they had thrown among the lumber in the courtyard.

"Perhaps that is it," said the physician. "At any rate, we can try it and see."

The horse was accordingly dragged out into the middle of the city square, where it was carefully examined and secretly put in order by the physician. A circle was then drawn around it upon the ground, and in this circle the physician placed a number of chafing-dishes with a little fire burning in each. The princess, closely veiled, was then led into the charmed circle, and while the sultan and the great men of Kashmir stood around, Firouz Schah lifted her into the saddle. He then threw some chemicals into the chafing-dishes, and immediately so dense a smoke arose that no one could see through it; but a moment afterward the sultan, lifting his eyes, saw the enchanted horse sailing through the sky with Firouz Schah and the princess upon his back.

"Sultan of Kashmir," cried a voice from above, "when next thou wouldst wed a princess, be sure to obtain her consent!"

Firouz Schah and his betrothed returned to Persia, where they lived happily together forever afterward.